Susan Titus Osborn
Marlene Bagnull
W. Terry Whalin
Mary Carpenter Reid
Gayle G. Roper
Donna Clark Goodrich
Christine Harder Tangvald
Lowell S. Saunders
Jessica Shaver
Lee Roddy
Mona Gansberg Hodgson

THE COMPLETE GUIDE TO

Christian Writing and Speaking

Kathy Collard Miller
Nancy I. Sanders
Dennis E. Hensley
Cecil Murphey
Carole Gift Page
Sally E. Stuart
Marita Littauer

Second Edition

Susan Titus Osborn,
General Editor

Write Now Publications
Phoenix, Arizona 85013

The Complete Guide to Christian Writing and Speaking, Second Edition

Cover design by Eric Walljasper
Interior design by Pine Hill Graphics

The original edition of this book was published by Promise Publishing Company, Orange, California.

Published by WriteNow Publications (a division of ACW Press)
5501 N. 7th, #502, Phoenix, AZ 85013

Publisher's Cataloging-in Publication
(Provided by Quality Books, Inc.)

The complete guide to Christian writing and speaking /
Susan Titus Osborn, general editor. -- 2nd. ed.
p. cm.
ISBN: 1-892525-60-7

1. Christian literature--Authorship--Handbooks, manuals, etc. 2. Public speaking--Religious aspects--Christianity--Handbooks, manuals, etc. 3. Christian literature--Publication and distribution. I. Osborn, Susan Titus, 1944-

BR117.C66 2001 808'.06623
QBI01-200921

Printed in the United States of America.

Contents

Introduction

"We need a Christian handbook for beginning and advanced writers and speakers written by the top experts in the field." These words are spoken over and over at writers' conferences and speakers' seminars. The same need is expressed in letters to *The Christian Communicator* and to the Christian Communicator Manuscript Critique Service.

To meet this need, an expert from each genre of Christian writing was chosen to provide a chapter or two in a specialized area of writing or speaking. As a result, this book begins with the basics for the individual who has never written and continues through advanced discussions on book contracts and tips for polishing speeches. Magazine articles, fillers, poetry, autobiographical writing, picture books, first chapter books, juvenile novels, adult novels, and nonfiction books are covered. Other chapters include practical information such as copyright law, interviewing techniques, marketing your manuscripts, time management, and the business side of both writing and speaking.

All individuals, who are interested in writing and/or speaking, will find something of value in these pages. Whether you are a beginning writer with a wish to glorify God with your writing, an intermediate writer with an urge to make the transition from writing articles and short stories to writing books, or a speaker with a desire to fine-tune your presentations or write a book to enhance your ministry, this book is for you.

People often ask if they have enough talent to write or to speak. A general consensus of the contributing authors of this book says that talent plays a minor role in the writing process. Writing is mostly hard work. Finding an idea, making an outline, and developing the first rough draft are the easy steps. The difficult part is *rewriting, rewriting, and rewriting*—polishing your manuscript until it is the best you are capable of writing. In public speaking, it is important to learn to give your speech from a well-written outline.

Bill Anderson, president of the Christian Booksellers Association (CBA), says, "Average is just as close to the bottom as it is to the top." Do not allow your writing and speaking to be average. God and your readers deserve your best.

People in today's society are searching for meaning in their lives. America is hungry for spiritual fulfillment. We can meet these needs with the power of our pens and our presentations, but only when our thoughts, ideas, and words reflect God's thoughts. Write with love. Write good literature. Write what Jesus would write if He held your pen or sat at your computer today.

After reading this book we invite you in joining us in implementing the Writers' Creed: When you are learning, seek help. When you are published, pass it on.

Giving help to others who are learning the crafts of writing and speaking across America and around the world is one of the major goals of the contributing authors of this book.

1 Write It Right!

by Susan Titus Osborn

You never get a second opportunity to make a good first impression.

—Mark Twain

The first impression an editor receives of you, the writer, is the manuscript you submit. This chapter contains what you need to know to present a professional looking manuscript for an article or story to a publishing house. Learn where to begin, how to begin, and where to go from there. You want to write, to get published, and to glorify God, so "Write It Right!"

Why are you writing? Is it to share your story with others? Are you seeking personal growth? Is it a ministry? Is it to make money? Making a living as a freelance writer is extremely difficult. Hopefully, your *main* purpose for writing is to provide a ministry. Personally, I want to change lives and to share something with others that will benefit them.

Decide what time commitment you are willing to make. Be aware that you can't wait until everything else is taken care of to start writing. Writing needs to become a priority, and it is demanding of your time and energy. Other things may have to be sacrificed to gain the hours you plan to devote to writing.

The important thing is to set aside a certain amount of time to perfect your craft. You can either designate large blocks of time—if you have them—or you can write for a few minutes a day. However, you must be committed to whatever time you set aside, and it must be quality time. Also, you need to find a quiet place, free from interruption. It helps if you can write at the same time every day.

Always pray for God's guidance before you start writing. We must listen to God and submit to His will before we can start writing for Him effectively.

Writing Goals

Perhaps it would be helpful for you to establish personal writing goals. If you write one story or article a month, at the end of a year you will have twelve articles or stories. If you are unpublished, I do not recommend that you begin with books. Start with articles or short stories. Write down what time commitment you are willing to make and pray about it.

It might help you to set up a goal sheet and answer the following five questions:

1. What is your overall purpose in writing?
2. What are some actions you can take that will help you make writing a priority?
3. How much time are you willing to commit to writing a day to achieve your writing objectives?
4. What are your realistic writing goals for the next year?
5. What are your writing goals for the next five years?

Now let's turn our attention to the writing process.

The Three-Step Writing Method

First Step: Theme and Outline

Before you begin to write your article or story, decide what your primary purpose is. The first step in the writing process is to state your theme in one word. Then state it in one sentence. Do this for short pieces, devotionals, stories, and articles, as well as for books. Each point must support the main theme.

Another way to look at this is to say that your article or story must have focus. Focus is deciding on a general theme or premise and developing it throughout the piece. Most articles are rejected because the writer deviates from the premise or tries to tell too many stories in one article. One idea, well developed and remembered by the reader, is worth more than many thoughts read and forgotten.

Next, create a preliminary outline before you write one word of the actual manuscript. Set up headings for the points you want to cover in your article and subheadings if you think of them. This outline is only for your use, so it doesn't have to be fancy or follow exact rules.

After your outline is written, finish the first stage of writing your article, which is to develop your idea into a full page. Accomplish this task by using the analytical, or critical, side of your brain. First, get your ideas down on paper. Writing style shouldn't be a concern at this point.

An alternative to creating an outline is to use the "Wheel Method." Draw a circle in the middle of a page and write your theme in the center. Draw spokes emanating from the circle, and write concise thoughts about your theme. Do this in any order that thoughts come. After formulating as many thoughts about your main theme as you can, arrange your thoughts in logical order to form an outline.

Second Step: Rough Draft

After finishing your outline, wait a few days before you begin the second step of the writing process, which is to write the first rough draft of your article or story. As you begin, let the theme and supporting ideas form in your mind.

Now, write your story. Turn off the critical side of your brain, and turn on the creative side. Let the words flow onto the paper. Don't get hung up on spelling, punctuation, or phraseology; just write whatever comes to your mind. Try not to think about your outline or theme sentence. Write the first draft in one sitting. Pick a location and time to write that will allow for a minimum of interruption.

Get everything down on paper you can think of regarding your subject. You may end up with enough material for several articles. Don't worry about that while writing this first draft, or you may not have enough material. If you're short of words, you'll need to go back and add more information during the editing stage.

Third Step: Rewriting

Writing the first draft is the creative part. For me, this is the fun part. The hard part is rewriting, rewriting, and rewriting. What separates those who become published writers from those who would like to be writers is a willingness to work through this process of polishing their work step by step. Polishing is always hard work, but the shine that results is worth the effort.

Your first stories, articles, or books may take a long time, but you will learn from practice. Even if it takes one hundred hours to write your first article, it is not wasted time. You will learn valuable lessons to apply to future writing, which will most likely flow smoother.

After you have written your first draft, set it aside for at least a week. It is easy to become so enthused about your first draft that you are convinced it is ready for publication. Chances are, however, it is not.

When you pick up your manuscript for the third time, you've put some distance between your emotions and your work, and you are ready to begin the third step of the writing process. This involves editing your own work. Now you should be able to look at it more objectively. You can treat it like a jigsaw puzzle, rearranging some of the pieces to make them fit better.

First read through your first draft for an overview. Make a mark in the margin where it doesn't flow smoothly. Read quickly. Don't stop and ponder what is wrong. That will come later when you do the line-by-line editing.

Then go back and look at your outline and theme sentence. Do they need revision? Does your article or story support your outline and theme? If not, you need to change either your theme and outline or your first rough draft. Remember, *nothing* is set in concrete at this stage. Ask yourself the following questions:

Twelve Evaluation Questions

1. Do I have a good beginning?
2. Is my story or article interesting?

3. Is it significant?
4. Is my story or article marketable?
5. Does it have continuity?
6. Does it make sense?
7. Have I left out any important points?
8. Did I say what I wanted to say?
9. Do my paragraphs flow smoothly?
10. Did I repeat my thoughts?
11. Did I use complete sentences?
12. Does my ending tie into my beginning?

Now look at the opening sentence and paragraph. Do you hook the reader with your opening? Does it make the reader want to continue reading? Beginnings, for me, are the most difficult part of a manuscript to write. Often I end up throwing out the first three paragraphs or even the first page. Don't struggle too long on your beginning at this point. You can always come back and edit it on subsequent drafts. Or, you may prefer to start with the "middle" and go back to write the beginning later.

After you have followed these steps, go through your article, carefully looking for spelling errors, missing punctuation, and incorrect grammar usage. Tighten your writing by eliminating unnecessary words. Rearrange the paragraphs and sentences to make your writing flow smoothly. Become familiar with books such as *Elements of Style* (by William Strunk Jr. and E.B. White) in order to learn the mechanics of grammar, punctuation, and word usage.

Writing is hard work. The words we put down on paper come from deep within us, and they are part of us. However, some of these words need to be rewritten, edited, or deleted entirely.

Twenty-eight Pitfalls

When you critique the first draft of your manuscript, watch for the following pitfalls:

1. Watch for Impractical Vocabulary

Don't talk down to your reader, and don't talk above his or her head. *Reader's Digest* and *Guideposts* are written on a sixth-grade level.

Keep your writing on a parallel level with your reader. Use "ten cent" words rather than words not commonly used in conversation. You can express profound thoughts and still write in a clear manner.

2. *Watch for Unnecessary Words*

Eliminate any words, sentences, or paragraphs that don't further your story line. Go through your manuscript word by word and ask yourself, "What will happen if I leave that out?" If the answer is "nothing," then cut it.

3. *Watch for Unnatural Speech*

Your words should flow in a conversational manner as if you were sitting at your dining room table having a cup of tea with a friend. Make your words sound natural. You will be able to do this with practice and lots of rewriting.

4. *Watch for Long, Run-on Sentences*

If the reader drowns in your sentences, he will feel lost. Keep your writing simple. That doesn't mean the content is simple, but the style is. When a sentence is shorter, it usually becomes stronger. Try to keep your sentences under twenty-five words.

5. *Watch for Monotonous Sentences*

Have you ever gone to a boring lecture where the speaker droned on in a monotone? Perhaps it was the lecturer's tone that put you to sleep. Since your readers can't hear you, change your tone by varying the length of your sentences. Also vary the structure of your sentences.

6. *Watch for Unclear Material*

Sentences that don't flow well can be detected by reading them aloud. Also, have someone else read your manuscript and edit it. I cannot emphasize enough the importance of belonging to a critique group. Form one with local writers in your area and meet regularly.

7. *Watch for Incongruities*

If you are writing a historical story set during World War II, don't have the characters watch television. It wasn't invented yet. Also, many words came into our vocabulary after World War II. Check to see when a word came into use if there is any doubt in your mind.

8. *Watch for Loose Ends*

Did you drop a character in your story? If you edit out a character or a piece of furniture, don't let it pop up later. People who aren't as close to your story as you are will be able to see loose ends better than you will.

9. *Watch for Digression*

Irrelevant material should be eliminated. Remove needless descriptions of people and places. Ask yourself if a scene is necessary. If not, delete it. Use judgment in deciding which characters should be described and in how much detail, what facts are relevant, and what can be left out.

10. *Watch for Put-downs*

You don't want to offend any element of your audience. Flippant remarks stand out. Watch your own personal prejudices regarding race, sex, and age, and try not to let them creep into your writing. Keep your writing broad-based so it will appeal to a wide audience.

11. *Watch for Flashbacks*

Use flashbacks sparingly, and don't flashback on flashbacks. They are tricky, and you don't want to lose your readers. Carefully take the readers back to an exact time and place, then bring them forward with good transitions and perhaps some telescoping narrative (covering a long period of time in few words).

12. *Watch for Abstract Words and Concepts*

Use concrete words instead of abstract ones. Strangely, you may find it more difficult to write simply, in descriptive concrete terms, than to express complex thoughts. People tend to think in the abstract. Put as much detail and description in as is feasible.

13. *Watch for Christian Clichés*

Don't use Christian jargon that pigeonholes you into one market. Examples are: "washed in the blood" or "born-again Christian." Try to avoid any terms that are not found in the Bible. You will find "born again" in the Bible, but you won't find "born-again Christian."

Christianese keeps you from crossing over into denominations other than your own. More importantly, its use keeps you from being effective with non-Christians. Non-Christians will often pick up a Christian magazine or book, especially when they are dealing with a problem. Your writing may be able to reach out and touch these individuals and perhaps bring them to Christ. Write so they can understand your words.

14. Watch for any Clichés or Jargon

Avoid clichés like the plague, and don't be caught dead using them. They are old hat and will bore your audience to tears. Likewise, don't use shoptalk or jargon only understood by one segment of the population, such as legalese and medical terms.

15. Watch for Humdrum Verbs

Use action verbs. The verb is the most important part of the sentence. It moves the reader along. For instance, look at the dynamic verbs for movement starting with S: Strut, skip, slink, smash, stomp, slither, stumble, stagger, sashay, swagger, step, stalk, straddle, slip, sneak, steal, slide, shadow, stamp, skid, and stride. Aren't these more exciting than "walk"? Use dynamic, descriptive verbs.

Use onomatopoeia, words that imitate sounds. These are especially effective when writing for children. Young children love to say words that sound like what they are. Splish, splash, whirl, crash, crunch, smash, growl, and buzz are examples. Plus, they are all dynamic verbs.

16. Watch for Passive Voice

Keep your sentences in the active voice, with the subject doing the acting rather than being acted upon. "The car slammed into the man" is more powerful than "The man was hit by the car." Keep the readers involved in what is happening.

17. Watch for "To Be" Verbs

Eliminate weak verbs such as "was," "were," "is," "had," "have," "become," and any form of "to be." Instead of writing "He is happy," use

"He skipped down the road humming his favorite tune." Often when you eliminate a "to be" verb, you also get rid of an "ing." Example: Instead of saying, "The man was ambling down the road," use "The man ambled down the road."

18. Watch for Negatives

Write in a positive form. Leaving out negative words makes your writing clearer and more upbeat. Also, negatives are often confusing. Example: Instead of saying, "He was not very often on time," say, "He usually came late."

19. Watch for Abstract Nouns

Use descriptive nouns. Nouns that are concrete, specific, and definite are best. Instead of "tree," name a type that describes what you want the reader to see: eucalyptus, magnolia, or aspen.

20. Watch for Adjectives

Adjectives are necessary, but use them sparingly. An overdone example is: "The thin, narrow black ribbon of highway wound through the velvety, emerald-green dense jungle that lurked on either side of the thin, narrow black ribbon of highway." Instead say: "The narrow ribbon of highway wound through the dense jungle that lurked on either side."

21. Watch for Adverbs

Instead of using a weak verb and an adverb, use a dynamic verb in the past tense. Instead of "walked slowly," use "ambled." By using strong verbs, you can eliminate most adverbs.

22. Watch for Tags

"He said" is a perfectly good tag and can be used often. It is usually better than "he uttered," "he articulated," or "he expressed." What matters is what he said, i.e., the words within the quotation marks. You can use an occasional word like whispered, shouted, or asked, but try to keep your tags in dialogue simple. Sometimes you can eliminate them altogether if it is obvious who is speaking.

23. *Watch for Noncommittal Language*

Avoid tame, colorless, hesitant, or noncommittal language. Try not to use words such as "little," "so," "very," "just," and most "thats." Keep your readers interested in what you are saying by the way you say it.

24. *Watch for Preachy Words*

"Would," "should," "could," "may," "might," and "can" should be used sparingly. If you preach to your audience, you will lose them. Jesus didn't tell people what to do, nor did He use abstract concepts. He spoke in parables. He used anecdotal stories to get His points across to His audience. Try using that same technique.

25. *Watch for Missing Punctuation*

Make sure that your commas are in the right places and that none have been left out. Do you have a period or other punctuation at the end of each sentence? A good reference for proper punctuation is Strunk and White's *Elements of Style.*

26. *Watch for Cumbersome Punctuation*

Be careful not to overpunctuate with commas. Today we use fewer commas than in the past. Also avoid the overuse of dashes, exclamation points, semi-colons, and colons.

27. *Watch for Poor Transitions*

Your paragraphs must flow into each other. If the transition seems rough, add an introductory clause or phrase to smooth it out. "After several hours of traveling, we arrived," or "When we reached Phoenix, we were greeted by our host."

28. *Watch for Telling*

Show, don't tell. On first rough drafts, writers often tell the story in narrative either from an observer's viewpoint or from the main character's mind. Both of these locations are boring. Readers want to participate in the action. They want to join in the excitement and experience the events as they are happening.

Be concrete, specific, and definite. Use dialogue, anecdotes, and fictional techniques whether you are writing fiction or nonfiction. When we avoid these twenty-eight pitfalls, we make our writing come alive. This is how we can truly reach our readers and touch their lives.

After several rewrites, when you feel that your article or story is as good as you can make it, then it is time to have other people read it. Belonging to a critique group is an essential part of the writing process. Find a group of writers in your area and meet with them on a regular basis.

Read all the books and magazines you have time for. I feel it is necessary to read as many hours as you write. You have to pour in, or there is nothing to pour out. Pick up all the freebies available at conferences. Subscribe to writers' magazines such as *The Christian Communicator, Writer's Digest,* and *The Writer.*

You can create your own letterhead stationery on a computer by using special fonts and a laser printer. You can also create your own business cards. Blank stationary and business cards are available at an office supply store.

Manuscript Submissions

Now you are ready to type your article in final form and send it to a publisher. Use the following format (pictured on the following page): Your manuscript should be double-spaced on white, 20 lb. paper with 1 to 1-1/2 inch margins. It is permissible to use computer or photocopying paper, but send a *clean* copy. Use Courier, Courier New, or Times New Roman font in 12-point type. Leave the right margin unjustified (ragged). The preset standard margins on a computer are acceptable. Put a header and page number on each page except the first.

Left Heading

Always put your name, address, telephone number, and e-mail address if you have one on the top left corner of the first page of the manuscript. If an editor needs to call you, he has your phone number at his fingertips.

Sample First Page for Article or Short Story Manuscript

Susan Titus Osborn
3133 Puente Street
Fullerton, CA 92835
714-990-1532
Susanosb@aol.com

First Rights
About 1200 Words
© 2000 Susan Osborn
SS# 521-00-0000

The Fire

by Susan Titus Osborn

"Mom, I had to abandon my car." My son sounded breathless and desperate at the other end of the telephone line. "Flames were jumping across the highway. Burning branches fell into the backseat of my convertible."

"Are you OK?" I asked.

Right Heading

To maintain balance, these are the four items that go in the top right corner of the first page:

1. Rights

On the first line, list which rights you are offering. Normally if this is the first time you are selling your article or story, you will offer "First Rights." This gives an editor one-time rights to publish your material before you offer it to another publication. *Do not* offer your article or story elsewhere until after it comes out in print the first time if you sold first rights.

Once your article or story is printed by the publication to which you first sold it, then you may sell second or "Reprint Rights." Copies of this same manuscript can be sent simultaneously to many different publications, but make sure they don't have overlapping audiences.

2. Word Count

On the second line, write the approximate number of words. If your article or story is more than 500 words, round off to the nearest hundred words. If it is under 500 words, estimate to the nearest fifty words.

3. Copyright

The third line is for your copyright information. Make a copyright symbol by choosing the appropriate keystroke on your computer. This is followed by the year and your legal name.

4. Social Security Number

Your social security number goes on the fourth line. A publisher cannot pay you unless he has this number. Your check may be delayed if an editor has to ask you for it at a later date. At the end of the year, you will receive a 1099 income tax form stating your income from each publisher—if your royalties are high enough. The Internal Revenue Service requires a 1099 form if your income was over $600 from any given publisher.

Subsequent Pages

Use a header with your last name and a key word from the title in the top left hand corner of the second and all following pages. Put the page number in the top right corner of all but the first page.

Make a second copy of your manuscript. Never mail your only copy, and *never* fold a manuscript. Place it in a 9 x 12 manila envelope or a Priority Mail envelope. Include another folded 9 x 12 self-addressed, stamped envelope (SASE) if you want your manuscript returned, or include your email address or a self-addressed, stamped postcard if you don't want the manuscript returned. Before you mail your manuscript, make a list of all the publishing houses that might consider buying it.

Mail your manuscript to a specific editor, not just to a publishing house. If you've met an editor at a conference, it helps considerably. Mention that person by name in your cover or query letter. Remember to look in the marketing guide to see if that publication wants a query letter or the entire manuscript. Most magazines and take-home papers pay on acceptance, but a few pay on publication.

Some of you will publish books someday, but it probably will be necessary to first serve an apprenticeship. Others will write articles and stories. Many are called to write, but not all are chosen to be professional writers. Some may be called to write for church newsletters. Other individuals may find a ministry of writing personal letters to friends, relatives, or missionaries. This kind of writing often changes lives. A few of you may find that writing isn't what God had in mind for you after all. That's OK, too.

As you begin your writing careers, remember that God is in charge. He has given each of us special talents which He expects us to use to glorify His name. Help your readers to get in tune with themselves through the experience of reading what you write. If you can help others get in touch with their own feelings and in touch with God, then God has truly used you as His divine instrument.

Write that Magazine Article 2

by W. Terry Whalin

I write for a couple of hours every day. Even if I only get a couple of sentences I put in that time. You do that every day, and inspiration will come along.

—Dave Barry

You roll the paper into the typewriter and sit poised with your hands on the keys, staring at the blank page. Or, maybe you turn on your computer and sit, watching an empty screen. What do you write?

Many writers and would-be writers have told me how that blank page petrifies them. In this chapter, we'll explore my technique for putting together a magazine article from idea to finished product.

Getting Over the Hump

I rarely have trouble putting those initial words on paper because I always do some preparation ahead of time, and then I use a simple trick, which I'll share with you in this chapter.

Ideas for magazine articles are everywhere, and the periodicals to write for are just as plentiful. Maybe you have an interesting personal experience story to relate. Possibly you have been involved in a ministry and created some unique materials you'd like to tell about in a how-to article. Maybe you've compiled some teaching on a topic from the Bible and want to get that into print.

Or, if you don't have any material from your own experiences to write about, consider interviewing interesting people around you and writing their stories for publication.

The first question to ask is: What publication will use this article? The possibilities are endless: adult, women, men, children, teenagers, or youth. Then ask: Who is my audience? Are they in a specialized occupation such as pastors or schoolteachers? Are they a certain age? The important thing is to be sure to target a specific audience—not just Christians in general.

However, every writer meets with rejection and has projects that are never published. I caution you that rejection and unpublished articles are a part of the writer's life and the road to consistent publication.

Assignment: Increasing the Odds of Publication

The bulk of my magazine writing is done on assignment, but how do you get an assignment?

Which magazines do you read on a consistent basis? Your familiarity with these publications and the types of articles they publish give you some needed background.

Pull out the magazines that come into your home. Organize them, including several months from the same publication. Then study the contents. What types of articles do they publish? How-to articles? Personal experience? For example, at *Decision*, where I was Associate Editor, almost every article is a first person, personal experience story. If you send a how-to article which is not written in the first person, you are asking for rejection. Or, if you write a story about someone else in the third-person, you will again invite rejection.

After you have studied the publications, write for their writers' guidelines. Almost every magazine has guidelines for authors. If these are not available on the publication's Web site, write a simple letter asking for guidelines and enclose a self-addressed, stamped envelope for the response. You can usually find the address for the publication on the masthead of the magazine under editorial offices or consult a market guide.

After reading through the guidelines, you will have some additional information. Does the publication accept query letters or prefer full manuscripts? Some magazines have a query only system. This means that you have to write a query letter and get a letter of request from the editor *before* sending the full manuscript. Other publications do not look at query letters but only completed manuscripts.

What's a query letter? Entire books have been written on this topic, and one of the best is *Irresistible Query Letters* by Lisa Collier Cool (Writer's Digest Books). A query is a single-page letter that sells your story idea. It has a four-paragraph formula. The first paragraph is the creative beginning for your article, *if* that explains your article. Otherwise summarize your article in a paragraph. The purpose of this first paragraph is simply to capture the editor's attention.

I won't walk you through the day of an editor, but since I've been one for years, I know they are involved in a multitude of tasks. An editor often reads query letters at the end of the day, late at night, or in a car pool on the way home. To capture his attention, your letter must be interesting.

The second paragraph includes the main points of how you will approach the article. The third paragraph gives your personal qualifications for this topic and your writing credits, if you have any. It basically answers the question: Why should you be the writer to get this assignment? Highlight your own area of expertise in this paragraph.

The final paragraph tells how soon you could write the article (for example: "Three weeks from assignment"). Be sure to allow yourself enough time. Also, state that you are enclosing a self-addressed, stamped envelope (SASE) and are looking forward to a reply. I often send the letter to as many as ten different publications at the same time.

Within the magazine business, there is an on-going discussion about simultaneous submissions—sending the exact same finished article to several publications. If you do this, you may end up on the black list of authors. Each publication has a list of people they will not work with. You don't want to be on that list. Also, each publication has a list of authors they use regularly and call with ideas for assignments. Your goal should be to get on the latter.

From my perspective, a simultaneous query letter is not the same as a finished article. Go ahead and query several magazines at the same time on the same topic if you think you can write several different articles on that same subject. One magazine may ask for 500 words on the topic while another may approach it from an entirely different viewpoint and ask for 2,000 words. Your illustrations and information will be considerably different. If you send the query to ten magazines, you may get ten rejections.

On the other hand, perhaps you will get an acceptance or two, or at least a request to see the entire article on speculation. "On speculation" means that the editor is not under obligation to purchase your article if it doesn't meet the periodical's standards.

I want to include some insight regarding why queries and manuscripts are rejected. An article or query may be rejected for many different reasons. Maybe the publication has already purchased an article on that topic. Perhaps an editor has recently assigned that subject to another author. Possibly the publication has an article on that topic appearing in an issue that is already in production but hasn't been printed. There are many different reasons for rejection that are out of your control as a writer and that have nothing to do with the quality of your writing.

Sometimes a new assignment can come as a result of a previous rejection. Several years ago, I queried a number of magazines about writing on listening to the Bible on tape. I targeted the January issues of publications for this short how-to article. Every magazine rejected it.

Several weeks later, I received a telephone call from a new editor at *Christian Life* magazine. That was one of the publications that had rejected the idea earlier. "We're sorting through some old queries," she explained. "Would you be able to write 500 words on the topic in the next three weeks?" No problem. That little article turned into one of my most popular articles for reprint in other publications.

After Deciding Your Topic

After you've decided on a publication and the type of article you are going to write, what happens next? It's time to begin your research. Accurate information is important to the credibility of your article. If you make an error, you will lose the respect of your audience.

However, let me give you one word of caution about research. Make sure you have a specific ending to your research. Some writers spend huge amounts of time in research and never sit down to write the article. How will you collect the information for your article? Will it come from your personal experiences? Will you need some stories from other people? Will it involve library or online research for statistics?

At your local library, make friends with the librarians. They are a gold mine of information and resources.

Sometimes a story will require interviewing one or several people. Prepare your questions before the interview. Also use a recording device for the actual interview. I have a small micro-cassette player, which is almost immediately forgotten by the person I'm interviewing. I've had people lean closer to me, forgetting the machine, and say, "I've never told this to anyone."

For some stories, the interview doesn't have to be long-even ten minutes on the telephone can get some useful stories and quotations—provided you're asking pointed questions.

Just remember these three points for interviewing:

1. No matter how famous the person, don't forget he is a real person with feelings and concerns. It will help you treat him naturally.
2. If it is a telephone interview, you have to tell the person that you are recording the conversation for legal purposes. Also, use a good recording device (ask your local Radio Shack dealer).
3. If the person is well known and seemingly unreachable, try asking his publisher to set up an interview. Explain your purpose and the amount of time you need. Most publishers are more than willing to help you schedule an interview with their authors. These publishers will furnish you with complimentary books as background for your research and schedule the interview time.

After the article is published, send, or arrange for the magazine to send, a copy of the article back to the publisher. Publicists for book publishing houses have dozens of projects going simultaneously. Your article will appear months after you set up the interview. Some of these interviews result in articles, and others do not. Establish your track record with the publishers for following through on your ideas and getting the information from their author published. This step of sending them the article builds your credibility and reputation as a writer for future writing projects.

After the Research

If you've written a query letter, then you've already written the opening for your article. Otherwise, the first step in the writing is to create an interesting opening story. The key is to make it motivating. The opening has to propel the reader into the rest of the article so he can't stop reading.

Here's one example from my own personal testimony: "I've gone to church most of my life, but I lived off my parent's faith until halfway through my sophomore year in college." Would that opening encourage you to keep reading?

Here's the way my actual testimony began in a published article, "I slapped the snooze alarm for the third time and finally opened my eyes at my Chi Phi fraternity house. Last night had been a late one. After covering an evening speech and interview for the school paper, I worked frantically on the story until just before midnight, when I dropped it into the hands of a waiting editor."

Compare these two examples. Notice the detail in the second version. I am not telling you about the experience; I am showing you. Repeatedly the writing books and teachers say, "Show, don't tell." They are saying to include dialogue and the type of detail for a story that will propel the reader into the article.

After writing the opening for the article, how do you continue? If you've done your research, you will have a target length for it. This word count helps give some definition to your plan.

Also, while gathering your research, hopefully, you've thought about the article and focused it. Can you summarize the point of the article into a single sentence? Complete the sentence: My article is about ______. After you've written this sentence, never wander away from this goal. When I was editing articles at *Decision*, sometimes the author would begin well, then wander around, and finally conclude. The articles lacked focus. The focus sentence statement will help you keep the article on track.

I write from an outline. Normally my article will have a number of points or illustrations. A standard outline would be the problem, the possible solutions, and your solution. If you're writing about a person, your outline might include different aspects of the person's life such as childhood, life before Christ, and life after Christ. Write out the main points of your outline. When I write a short story, I use the same approach. What is the beginning, middle, and ending? An outline keeps the writer focused on the goal of the article.

Also be realistic with yourself and your writing life. Can you only write for thirty minutes a day or maybe only ten minutes? Maybe you are motivated to write the entire article in one session? Possibly you write only one point from your outline during a session. Whatever your writing goal, the point is to write consistently and keep moving the article toward completion.

After you've written the article, put it away for a period of time. If you are on a tight deadline, that might only involve eating lunch and then returning to it. If you have the time, it might involve several days or a week. When you return to your article, read it out loud. The ear is less forgiving than the eye. Reading it out loud will point out areas for you to revise and rewrite. Good writing requires rewriting.

Here are some questions to consider: Does it make sense? Are there areas that are missing? Can you tell some of the stories with more detail and emotion? Is the article focused for the targeted publication? How about the ending? As a reader, how do you feel about it? Does it come to a logical conclusion and tie up the loose ends?

Try to look at your writing objectively through impersonal eyes. Consider the purpose of your article. Was it to motivate readers to action? Did it achieve its purpose?

Sweep through the article and check it for spelling and grammar mistakes. You'd be amazed to know how many articles are submitted for publication with typing errors and simple grammatical mistakes. As a writer, you want to present the best article possible. Give it an additional check.

If you have the opportunity, ask a friend or a fellow writer to read your article and give you feedback. One caution about this process. Ultimately you are in charge of the contents of the article that you will submit. Don't soak up criticism like a sponge but consider each comment. Does it have validity? If so, change it; if not, ignore it.

The final step is to submit your material to a publication. In your cover letter to the publication, explain your familiarity with the magazine. If you've been a subscriber for years and faithfully reading it, say so. Don't exaggerate but this familiarity shows your professional stance. Also, express your willingness to make changes in the direction of the story, as well as any other revisions. Maybe an editor will like your opening illustration but have a completely different direction for the article. If you've expressed willingness to revise, you will have an opportunity for publication. If you've said, "I wrote it and this is it," then you'll miss that opportunity. The professional stance is to show flexibility to the direction from an editor.

There are many excellent books on writing magazine articles. I recommend five. The first one listed below can be purchased at your local Christian bookstore. The rest can be found in secular bookstores or through your local library.

1. *An Introduction to Christian Writing* by Ethel Herr (Write Now Publications). This is a good basic Christian writing text with hands-on exercises at the end of every chapter.
2. *The Magazine Article, How to Think It, Plan It, Write It* by Peter P. Jacobi (Writer's Digest Books). Dr. Jacobi regularly teaches at Folio seminars, which is where editors of the major magazines obtain additional training. He teaches magazine writing at Indiana University.
3. *The Complete Idiot's Guide to Publishing Magazine Articles* by Sheree Bykofsky, Jennifer Basye Sander, and Lynne Rominger (Alpha Books). You may not want to face the word idiot in this title. Get over it. Every chapter in this book is packed with advice from handling contracts to locating markets to crafting a query letter to the realities of freelance work (like rejection). These seasoned freelancers have covered everything, so you should read and re-read this book.
4. *Effective Magazine Writing* by Roger C. Palms (Shaw). This seasoned editor spent twenty-two years as editor of Decision magazine and now teaches at various writers' conferences. His book is laced with practical wisdom about finding time to write, crafting the various parts of an article, and interviewing.

5. *Handbook of Magazine Article Writing* edited by Jean M. Fredette (Writer's Digest Books). Here, in one volume, is a compilation of some of the best articles about magazine writing from past issues of Writer's Digest magazine.

A Final Word

The ministry of writing for magazines has no formula. Each article is unique from a creative source—you the writer. However, there is an expected format for articles. Your manuscript needs to be presented in a professional manner—typed, double-spaced with good margins, etc. Some publications have a formula to be followed for a specific section of their magazine (word length, essential elements, etc.).

Each writer has to discover his place of ministry with words. The process of discovery takes initiative on your part to step out and try. Also, it involves receiving some rejection but still being persistent. Maybe you can't write teaching articles but you have a creative bent for reaching teenagers. This process of self-discovery and ministry begins with a single step. Take that step and begin to fill that blank page with words.

A short time ago, I received a letter from a prisoner who had read my biography about Rómulo Sauñe. Other times, I have received letters from children who have enjoyed my books. We'll never know the impact of our words and articles. As I read magazine articles, they motivate me to take action and to change. Your articles can have the same impact.

3 The Art of Interviewing

by Nancy I. Sanders

Writing allows us to turn the chaos into something beautiful, to frame selected moments in our lives, to uncover and to celebrate the organizing patterns of our existence.

—Lucy McCormick Calkins

Did an editor assign you the task of writing an article about "Shepherding the Flock," and you're not a pastor? Or do you want to write a book about "The Role of Women Within the Church," and you're a man? How will you ever conduct enough research to cover the personal experience you lack? Don't despair! Interview someone!

An interview provides you with valuable insight needed for your writing project. It adds a personal touch to your manuscript, making the data believable to your reader. An interview provides anecdotes and background information. It is a valuable tool for the writer.

Preparing for the Interview

Before you embark on an interview project, evaluate the situation. If the person's story discusses an issue that strikes a raw nerve within you, you may not be able to write an unbiased article. Interviews often unearth sensitive and personal information. Be careful of a conflict of interests.

Pray about the project. Ask God for guidance, wisdom, discernment, and a compassionate spirit. Pray that individuals will be inspired to develop a deeper relationship with God. This sets the priorities.

I frequently write down my prayer and clip it to the front of the folder containing the interview's information. Each time I open the file folder to work on my project, I see the prayer. I am reminded of my commitment to write as a servant of God.

Evaluate the interview's market potential. If you plan to develop an article for a specific magazine, query that magazine first. Suggesting that your proposed article be written on speculation increases the possibility of acceptance especially if you are a beginning writer.

A query helps you learn a magazine's current needs. Once I wanted to interview various women about their capacity as spiritual mothers within their church family. I thought the article would match one magazine's audience perfectly. After writing a query to the editor, however, she informed me that their magazine was in the middle of publishing a similar piece. Valuable time and energy weren't wasted trying to tailor my article to fit their format.

Once you receive a publisher's acceptance, find out how to contact the interviewee (This can be done in reverse order). For celebrities, call library reference personnel to locate a personal address or an agent's telephone number. You probably need to call a large main library. This search may lead you through several agencies. Celebrities change agents, and the books in the library may contain outdated information. Keep persevering. Another option is to check the Internet to see if the person has a Web site.

Call a magazine to ask how to reach a person featured in its issue. When I needed to contact Donna Douglas (Ellie Mae from "The Beverly Hillbillies" TV series), I telephoned the magazine that featured her story. I was given the name, address, and telephone number of the author who wrote the article. (Note: Each magazine utilizes a specific policy regarding divulging similar information.) I called this person.

Because of an agreement, she could not tell me Donna's number, but she volunteered to contact her for me.

Often interviews involve people who boast no claim to fame. You still need to use a professional attitude and proceed through appropriate channels. For background information in an article I was writing, I wanted to interview two teens who attended a community AIDS seminar. First, I called my friend who personally knew several families who attended the seminar. She initially contacted the parents and asked permission for me to interview their teens. After the parents felt comfortable about my project and my role as an interviewer, I called these young adults and gathered the information I needed. If I had called the families myself, I may not have been granted the interviews I wanted.

Depending on the project, determine your options for interviewing. If you live in California and plan to interview someone in Pennsylvania, your interview will probably occur over the telephone or via email or the mail. Remain flexible. Conditions may change as you plan to meet the needs of the interviewee. When I contacted Philip Yancey (author/editor), he agreed to be interviewed. However, due to his heavy travel schedule to Russia at the time, he asked that all communication take place through the mail.

Design an adaptable plan. When you initially contact the person or his agent, politely introduce yourself. Explain which publisher is interested in the interview. Mention whether publication is on speculation or a definite assignment. Discuss the possibilities of a written interview, telephone interview, or conducting the interview in person. Provide a rough time estimate on the length needed for the interview. A twenty-minute telephone interview usually provides enough information for a 1,000-word profile. This same profile would probably require an hour's worth of time in a person-to-person interview.

If you have a deadline to meet, explain the time frame in which you are working. Request a biographical information sheet or a publicity page. Ask the expert you plan to interview to provide you with a one-page résumé. This covers basic background information about awards, educational degrees, and titles of projects.

As you design your list of questions for the actual interview, don't include questions that can be answered by a biography or basic research. Develop questions the readers of your target publication want to ask. I also include a question that interests me. Focus on asking,

"What did you feel like when...?", "Why did you...?", or "How do you feel people were affected the time you...?" Ten to fifteen questions usually provide sufficient information for a 1000-word article. Conclude with a question such as, "Do you have any other comments, advice, or information you would like to add to our discussion?"

Conducting the Interview

Your appearance is important in a person-to-person interview. Dress professionally, but don't overdress. Soft, muted colors work best. Dress for the occasion. If I interview my husband's co-worker about her experience as a teacher with full-inclusion special education students, I would probably wear a basic dress. If I interview my parents' neighbor about his experience as a dairy farmer, a nice pair of jeans and a blouse would be fine.

Check to see that the tape recorder has new batteries and operates well. Carry a small note pad and two pens. Cover yourself by using both methods.

There may be times when the tape recorder fails. For one telephone interview, I plugged my tape recorder into the telephone and into the wall outlet. I called the interviewee. Pressing "record" on the machine, I conducted the interview. I wrote topical notes on my note pad during the interview. When finished, I hung up the telephone and tried to rewind the tape. It didn't move. Aghast, I discovered that I had plugged my tape recorder into a wall outlet controlled by a light switch. The light switch had been turned off. Fortunately, the interview lasted only fifteen minutes, but I learned my lesson. If minimal topical notes are simultaneously taken, most of the interview can be reconstructed immediately afterward.

Make certain to bring your list of questions. Pray before the interview to ask God for sensitivity and wisdom. Arrive at the interview promptly, but demonstrate courtesy if the interviewee is not prompt.

Treat stranger and acquaintance alike with the same friendly and polite professional attitude. Occasionally, the tape recorder will remain unused. In one circumstance, I needed to observe a children's storyteller for a curriculum book I was writing. All the arrangements were made through the coordinator of the program. On the morning of my scheduled observation, I walked into the preschool classroom carrying my tape recorder and note pad. The storyteller took one look at me and said nervously, "I don't do tape recorders." I smiled and put the machine away.

Create a conversational environment during the interview, but don't become too familiar. An interview assignment with singer/songwriter Cynthia Clawson for *Today's Christian Woman* took place around Christmas. I knew that Cynthia had children. At the beginning of our conversation, I simply asked her what she bought her children for Christmas. A short, delightful conversation followed. We both felt at ease by the time we began the interview.

Be sensitive to the person you interview. Remember that an interview is a conversation and not a cross-examination. Know when to ask questions that probe deeper into an issue and when to ease back and go on to the next question. You don't want to appear as a wolf circling around its prey, waiting for the kill. Your task is to encourage the person to share vulnerable tidbits about herself. You want the interviewee to feel safe with you and non-threatened. If she begins to share something that makes her feel too self-conscious, relate a similar short story of your own. Allow yourself to become vulnerable, too, as your relationship develops.

Listen carefully during the conversation and maintain good eye contact. Converse throughout the interview, but keep your remarks short. You want to let the interviewee talk in order to gain necessary information. Don't try to impress her with yourself. Strive to maintain a balance between her monologue and your brief contribution to the conversation. This encourages a confidential atmosphere.

If the subject rambles, gently stop her. Attempt to summarize what she is trying to say. Then lead her back to the focus of the interview.

Before you finish, check that you know the correct spelling of important names, organizations, or information she mentioned. Hand her your business card. Ask permission to call her briefly if more information is needed.

Sometimes interviews fail to provide adequate data. In one assignment I needed to write a profile about a particular man. He agreed to a written interview, so I mailed him a list of questions. He returned my questionnaire with very short, concise answers. I called him to ask further questions, but his answers remained brief. He simply wasn't talking.

My deadline approached, so I dug through my research material. I examined his biographical sheet and information about the company for which he worked. Quoting him as much as possible, I managed to write a comprehensive profile. Research compensated for the inadequacy of the actual interview.

Writing the Interview

Listen to the tape recorder and type the interview verbatim. This seems tedious and time-consuming, but it is vital. Every word is written for your review. When finished, add the tape to your files. Keep tapes and written records to protect yourself against potential legal claims.

Next, surround yourself with the information you collected. Include transcripts of interviews, library research, newspaper articles, and letters of correspondence with people involved in the project. Golden nuggets of information can even be gleaned from the interviewee's acceptance letter.

Include several copies of the magazine for which you are writing and letters of correspondence you maintained with the editors. Refer frequently to these magazines as you tailor your writing to fit their styles. The editors' letters help pinpoint the angle they want.

Read and reread all collected information. Consider different approaches to take within the manuscript. Pray and ask God to guide you with the project.

When you feel saturated with information, begin to write the outline. Determine the goal you want your manuscript to achieve. List all the points you want to make. Arrange the outline to advance the reader smoothly through your information so he can focus on the goal.

Now you are ready to write. Push aside all thoughts of inadequate ability to write. Forget about grammar, punctuation, repetition of words, and perfect writing skills. Just write. Follow the outline and write what comes to mind.

Depending on the type of manuscript, choose some quotations to use verbatim and others to rewrite as background information only. Political interviews or newspaper articles require literal quotations. Magazine articles or celebrity biographies utilize quotations to help develop a personality profile. The quotations can be changed, but the essence of the person's message needs to be retained. Also, know the publisher's policy on quotation usage. Some publishers require a release form from each person quoted directly. While writing, keep these guidelines in mind.

As you progress, mark off information that you utilize. Write and write and write until the project, or the section of the project, is completed.

Now push up your sleeves and grit your teeth. Prepare yourself to be your own worst critic. By doing this, you become your own best editor.

If necessary, rearrange the order of entire sections of information so the manuscript flows naturally. Check grammar, punctuation, spelling, and 101 other things that are important in the mechanics of writing. Make certain each paragraph is structured correctly. Check and recheck the manuscript again and again.

As you edit your own writing, work to erase your voice from shouting to the reader. This is especially important in a personality profile. The reader wants to know the interviewee, not you. Try to aim your writing so it is written in the same style and educated level of the interviewee. Use favorite words or mannerisms he might use.

A few years ago, I interviewed children's singer/songwriter Mary Rice Hopkins. When my two boys were young, I attended one of her children's concerts. Mary was folksy, full of energy, and geared to children. I tried to develop the interview style so that her personality shone through.

One of the goals in writing a personality profile should not be to pass out the published article to your friends and say, "Look at how good a writer I am!" Your goal should be that the person you interview will want to pass out the article to her friends and family, saying, "Hey, look at this! Didn't the author do a nice job writing about me?"

One time over the telephone I interviewed an editor who had just arrived home after a trip. She agreed to be interviewed that evening because she planned to leave the next day on another trip. Her answers were on the negative side, simply because she was tired. At the end of the conversation she commented, "I hope I don't sound too negative, I really do enjoy being an editor."

As I wrote her profile, I worked hard to glean through her comments and present them in a positive, encouraging way. I felt this was her heart's desire. After I wrote the article and sent it to her for her approval, she returned it with a letter. She wrote, "I think your manuscript is very helpful. It captures the burden that I have, and I think you have expressed it well. Thank you for letting me 'speak my mind.'"

After working hard to edit, perfect, hone, refine, and polish the manuscript, you are ready to finalize it. Write a strong hook for the beginning and a brief but definite conclusion for the end.

Conducting Your First Interview

The idea of conducting an interview makes some people nervous. The following is practical advice to help you gain experience and confidence.

Start by interviewing a friend. Learn how to feel at ease in a person-to-person interview with someone you know. I conducted my first person-to-person interview this way. I asked my friend about a forum she coordinated for the local church community. I conducted the interview in a professional manner as if I were talking to a celebrity: tape recorder usage, note taking, question asking, etc. I didn't feel nervous. It was an excellent experience for me.

If you want to learn how to conduct a telephone interview, also talk to a friend. You gain experience in working equipment that plugs the tape recorder into the telephone. Practice techniques of listening and note taking. Afterwards, listen to yourself on the tape recorder to check if you refrained from interrupting the interviewee or if your tone of voice appropriately conveyed the empathy you wished to portray. Whether interviewing a friend or a professional by telephone, you are required to tell that person that the interview is being recorded.

Another suggestion is to interview a friend with a written questionnaire. Include a cover letter stating your purpose and a self-addressed, stamped envelope (SASE). When your questionnaire is returned to you, evaluate the answers. Were the questions you developed able to encourage your friend to write interesting responses for an article? Revise the questionnaire as needed.

Interview techniques involve certain mechanics such as using a tape recorder, note taking, and writing skills. However, they also include good communication skills. If you desire to be a top-notch interviewer, practice your listening skills in everyday conversation with friends and family. Ask a friend about an important issue in his life. Probe gently, learning when to pause or when to contribute to the conversation. By doing this in your daily life, positive interview skills will develop. At a scheduled appointment, you will be able to create the atmosphere needed to obtain the information you want.

4 Good Techniques for Good Critiques

by Mary Carpenter Reid

The beautiful part of writing is that you don't have to get it right the first time, unlike, say, a brain surgeon.

—Robert Cromier

Critique rhymes with technique. It's a fun word, and writers love fun words. But what does it mean?

Criticism comes to mind. *Scrutiny. Faultfinding. Judgment. Verdict. Condemnation. Dissection.* Ouch! It begins to get downright uncomfortable.

For writers, however, the meaning goes beyond that analytical process of criticism, which sometimes infers harshness and uncaring comment. We, as Christian writers, consider the word *critique* synonymous with *evaluate*.

Let us focus on constructive—not destructive—action. May an honest helpful evaluation be our intent whenever we attempt a critique of any manuscript entrusted to us by a fellow author.

Our Own Material

The same goes for self-editing. Just as we generate all that honest, helpful evaluation for others, let us do the same for ourselves when we work and rework our own projects.

Perhaps you don't have writing colleagues on whom to rely for regular input to your creative efforts. Your entire "critique group" may consist of one person—and that person is you. The how-to methods of fine-tuning a manuscript described in this chapter are valid for polishing any manuscript, whether you're doing a critique of someone else's work or self-editing your own.

Remember, even if you are blessed with a top-notch, supportive critique group, your main source of evaluation will always be yourself. Use the following suggestions to supplement your own writer's sense as you self-edit your material.

The Link Between Fiction and Nonfiction

Good writing skills enrich any type of writing. In this chapter, fiction-related techniques are deliberately blended with those of nonfiction because using fiction-writing skills will improve nonfiction. Your knowledge of constructing believable dialogue can make your anecdotes pulse with life.

Your familiarity with story plotting can help you present nonfiction material in an interesting, organized fashion. The person who is aware of the way climactic scenes quickly tie up loose ends and bring novels to a close knows the importance of providing a satisfying conclusion to a nonfiction piece.

On the other hand, the nonfiction writer, accustomed to incorporating detail in factual accounts, will know the importance of including specific details in a poem or devotional when he evaluates it. The how-to writer who battles the difficult task of writing clear, complete instruction is likely to spot weak or confusing descriptive passages in a novel. The article writer who supports his premise with logic will expect logic in the short story he reads.

What Is a Critique Group Anyway?

Definition: A critique group is writers in regular contact for the purpose of evaluating each other's work. With that comes support, encouragement, and inspiration. At least, we hope that is an offshoot of any critique group, especially a Christian group.

Christian writers are largely unselfish and willing to assist fellow writers. After all, our ultimate goal is to produce good writing to promote godly principles.

How Does a Critique Group Work?

Critique groups vary widely in size and style. A typical one might meet in a home. Some groups gather in restaurants or public meeting rooms. Some consist of three or four members; others could be a dozen or more. Some bring work in progress to the meetings; others mail copies to members ahead of time.

A group I belonged to met around a dining room table in one member's home. There were usually four of us, plus an occasional visitor. Our writing projects varied, covering a wide spectrum from short poems to long book chapters. We would bring several copies of our material and put them on the table.

Then, working silently, each of us reviewed the work of every other person. We scribbled, drew pictures, wrote notes, corrected grammar, and generally marked up the copies. In case there weren't enough copies, and more than one reader worked on the same copy, we used various colors of ink. That helped the author to later identify who wrote what.

After everyone finished, we moved into a discussion, beginning with something like, "Well, what do you think about Mary's chapter tonight?" Each manuscript received this brief verbal review. Before breaking up, we set the date for our next meeting.

Diversity in People

Diversity of our members' abilities and experience increased the value and effectiveness of our group. We each wrote different types of material, aimed at a broad range of readers. A person who writes adult manuscripts can raise interesting questions about stories aimed at children. The practical how-to writer can tug a poetic dreamer back to earth in a hurry.

More than bringing diversified technical perspectives to this manuscript evaluation, members of our group differed in personality and background. One was bolder than the rest and knowledgeable in marketing. Another never failed to see the humorous twists in our material: she also pointed out ways our words might be misread. A member who was a Bible student caught words that veered off base spiritually. Another's strength seemed to be the basic craft of writing.

In short, the skills of each person multiplied the overall effectiveness of the group. We gained knowledge and encouragement from one another.

Some Rules for Success

Manuscripts may deal with resolving life-and-death matters, but a critique group doesn't resolve much of anything. Here are some suggestions to use in a critique group:

- Be honest but kind in your comments.
- Don't be overly vague. Use concrete examples.
- Keep it light. Draw happy faces.
- Search for something positive about every manuscript.
- Laud improvement.
- Be open-minded to what others say about your work.
- Participate. Write and submit to the group.
- Don't blow your own horn.

Remember, in evaluating another's work, never attempt to change something needlessly. Don't nit-pick. Don't argue. Don't rewrite. Let the author have his say.

Also remember, don't mindlessly accept the comments heaped on your own manuscript. Be aware of the evaluator's current mood. Perhaps his mail carrier brought him a disappointing rejection that day. Perhaps he hates all adverbs, not just yours. Maybe he agrees so heartily with the views expressed in your opinion piece that he doesn't care whether or not you're making good sense.

Participation in a critique group calls us to think in terms of both specific evaluation and general evaluation. Specifically, our task is to:

- Point out possible errors or potential problems in the content.

- Help the author to convey the meaning in a succinct and clear manner.

Beyond these responsibilities is the sometimes hazy area of general evaluation. Here we rely on our good judgment to comment on the quality and craftsmanship of a piece.

Procedure

What actually happens when you sit with poised pencil before hundreds of words, gathered into sentences, clustered into paragraphs, and assembled on pages? This is, after all, someone's treasured creation. Here are a few suggestions before you begin critiquing:

Pray

Pray that God will guide you to be helpful, to see important errors, and to give valuable suggestions. Ask Him to help you refrain from exaggerated praise that leads to complacency or false promise. Pray that He will help you refrain from harsh criticism dispatched to puff up your own ego, and that, when your own manuscript takes its turn in the spotlight, He will help you accept and evaluate the assessment of others.

Know Author's Intent

What is the type of writing: article, short story, novel chapter, devotional? Is it partial or complete? What is the targeted market: teen periodical, Sunday school take-home paper, historical romance? What is the age of the intended reader? Is the manuscript simply a learning exercise for the author or a pastime? Is it a journal entry, a character sketch, or a vignette?

Ask Yourself Questions

Read the first paragraph or even the first half page. Stop and consider, "Will the beginning grab the reader's interest?"

Even at this early point in the manuscript, you can make an extremely valuable assessment. As a reader new to the material, no matter how ignorant you feel about its subject, you probably can judge the opening better than the author. He knows what he's trying to say, but is he saying it?

Did the beginning immediately catch your attention? Did it set the stage for great things to follow? Do you want to keep reading more? In addition, the beginning should give you a good feel for the mood of the piece.

In fiction, you should gain an immediate sense of the setting—the time and place, or at least the era and a clue about the location. Does the beginning indicate an atmosphere of intrigue, humor, or deep drama? Or does it leave you wondering if something you thought was comical was meant to be that way? In nonfiction, does the tone suggest you are to be enlightened, instructed, or persuaded? Does the lead sentence (whether a startling fact, a question, or the first line of an anecdote) relate to what follows? Or is it merely a hook designed to blatantly grab attention while failing to provide a smooth entry into the main body of the material?

The opening of any piece can raise questions, but it shouldn't leave you so confused that you don't know where it's headed.

Notice as You Read

- Are the verbs active?
- Are the nouns specific?
- Does the dialogue sound natural?
- Is the speech consistent with the speaker and the situation?
- Do the characters seem real?
- Are they behaving rationally?
- Do you care what happens to them?
- Does the material flow smoothly?
- Is it well organized?
- Does it suit the age of the potential reader?
- Are there any taboos for its market?
- Is the nonfiction illustrated with anecdotes?
- Does the fiction plot seem logical?
- How are the paragraph and sentence lengths?
- Was the spelling and punctuation checked?
- Could the same thing be said using fewer words?

Keep Watching

Is the meaning clear? Is the writing concise?

Finally

Does this manuscript have value for the prospective reader? Does it meet a need for knowledge, explanation, comfort, humor, entertainment, inspiration, or any of the reasons a reader chooses to spend his time reading?

Before You Return the Manuscript

Note the strong points. Sometimes we get so caught up in what is wrong with a manuscript that we forget to notice what is good. Surely you can find places as you read to jot "Good," "Nice description," "I like this," or "Makes me want to read more." At the least, write an encouraging general comment, if no more than "You are working hard on this. Keep it up."

Writing Objectives

Under the guise of general evaluation, the specter of marketing often raises its wobbly head. Is the manuscript appropriate for its intended market? Is it ready to compete with the thousands of others that cross the thresholds of publishing houses? It doesn't have to be. All of us are constantly learning our craft. Some writers aren't ready to submit to the publishing world. Some don't want to. That doesn't make their work any less worthy of our best evaluation.

As you grow familiar with your fellow writers, certain of their strengths will come to light. Encourage those strengths. In your opinion, the dialogue in Miss Storyteller's fiction always sounds as flat as the paper it's written on. Then one evening, Miss Storyteller shyly presents a copy of a devotional she has written. It positively sings with rhythm and with spirit. You suspect Miss Storyteller is brimming with devotional material. Suggest she do more in that field. Bring a book of devotionals to the next meeting to underscore their importance in Christian writing. Without discouraging the fiction writing, you're encouraging another outlet for your friend's creativity.

Problems in a Group

What about the person who prefers to talk about writing rather than to actually write? This person rarely brings in work. He probably doesn't offer much written evaluation of members' manuscripts, but he shines in the general discussion.

This situation will likely resolve itself when the talker finally gets bored in the company of serious writers and drops out. If he contributes constructive comments, there's no harm done. Simply set ground rules that keep any person from monopolizing the evening's discussion, or from chatting away while everyone else is trying to concentrate on the written words.

What about a person with a habit of making remarks that cut? We writers generally are fairly sensitive. If only one person has this nasty habit, perhaps everyone else can overlook it. Maybe a well-placed defensive comment can neutralize the barb. Possibly your group will be blessed with one of those rare individuals possessing a gift of lighthearted gab that warms an icy silence and defuses potential conflict.

Distributing a printed list of guidelines for kindness in critiquing might help, but only if the guilty party recognizes his guilt. Begin your meeting with a prayer that stresses the reason for your group's existence—to promote good Christian writing, not to boost individual egos by trampling on others'. It may take a friendly but frank heart-to-heart talk with the offender.

However you choose to handle the situation, remember that if one member constantly makes demeaning or cutting remarks, sooner or later, even the nicest people will answer back. Don't let your critique sessions evolve into scheduled arguments.

Going Solo

For the writer revising his own work, most of these group critique techniques can be used in the sometimes bewildering process of self-editing.

You *always* need to polish your own work. Even if you have the advantage of regularly attending a critique group, you'll benefit by submitting manuscripts that are reasonably clean. Don't give your fellow writers the easy task of highlighting conspicuous problems. You should find and correct them beforehand. A certain amount of time will be devoted to surveying your work. That time can be better utilized if the members' minds aren't consumed with minor matters you could have remedied yourself. Take advantage of the group's expertise by making it dig for obscure faults or serious shortcomings. Grant it the freedom to see the structure, the flow, and the impact.

When editing your own work, take a two-stage approach. First, read it aloud. Have your pencil in hand. Listen carefully. Invoke the self-discipline we are famous for and pause only long enough to put a check or brief notation by possible problem areas that occur to you as you read.

In this reading, try to catch obvious errors such as a slip in logic or in character viewpoint. A single viewpoint is the simplest. Even here, it is easy to wander. Make sure your viewpoint character doesn't know more than he should. Let him think, act, and speak based on only what he is able to assume, know, hear, or see up to that moment.

Watch for areas of dullness or repetition. How many times did you indicate a character's emotion by relying on his eyes widening, falling to the floor, blinking, staring, or darting somewhere?

Be on the lookout for mysterious strangers who wander cross your pages. If you begin a profile on Ed as a summer camp director, will the reader recognize Ed when, halfway through the article, you call him "Mr. Jones" or "the track coach from Western High"?

Notice the overall structure. Does your article have a clear premise? Is that premise supported? Have you unintentionally interjected points that don't pertain to the main subject matter?

In the second reading, go over the material bit by bit, paying particular attention to the previously checked areas. Make corrections and improvements to words and passages.

Often these corrections and improvements mean changes that necessitate making corresponding changes in other sections. Details such as hair style, eye color, and automobile model add richness to a story but can be a headache if you decide in Chapter Seven that a four-wheel drive fits the protagonist's personality better than the four-door he had in Chapter One. If you write an article suggesting ways to minister to shut-ins and then decide to focus on the more narrow area of convalescent home residents, be sure your final version has eliminated early ideas that are now unsuited to the more limited subject.

Sometimes it seems the changes never end. I rewrote the first chapter of my first book at least forty times. Put your manuscript away when you reach the end or a good stopping point, depending on the length. After it is cold, not just chilly, begin the process again from a fresh perspective. Chances are you'll find many more places that need changing. It's likely, too, that some of the penciled revisions you previously labored over will now fail to make as much sense as the original version did.

Although it's difficult to catch weaknesses and flaws in one's own manuscript, the more you work at the writing and rewriting, the better writer you will become.

A Compelling Reason

Much trash and much merit exist in the world to compete with Christian thoughts and actions. As writers, we owe it to our profession and to our self-respect to strive to write material that stands tall beside any commodity in the publishing industry.

At times, we may feel overwhelmed. More likely we picture ourselves as "Davids walking among Goliaths." However, we can make certain that our efforts are polished and our aims are unselfish. Let's strive to make our writing inviting to other Christians. Where appropriate, let's also make it of such appealing quality that the non-Christian will be drawn to it, unable to put it down until the telling of God's principles has worked a change in him.

Let's keep sight of our objective: Produce excellent writing that furthers God's words and God's ways.

5 Writing Fillers

by Mona Gansberg Hodgson

The writer's opportunity is to lean over to the reader's ear and say, "I have something to tell you."

—Loretta M. Wadsworth

Like a salad, fillers can serve as main courses, hors d'oeuvres to other writing, or as side dishes. Are you looking for a way to get your name in print? Are you seeking a diversion while you take a break from longer projects? Fillers are the dish I recommend.

Sometimes referred to as shorts, fillers usually take the shape of mini-articles in various forms up to 800 words, small humorous or informative items of fewer than 250 words, recipes, funny stories, children's bright sayings, devotionals, jokes, tips, cartoons, book reviews, poems, puzzles, witty sentences, sidebars, columns, and anecdotes of all kinds. Some publishers refer to anything fewer than 1,000 words as a filler.

Fillers appeal to both writers and editors.

Writers Like Fillers Because...

- They usually take less time to compose than full-length articles, so you have a finished project sooner.
- They offer good exercise in writing tight and concise.
- Because there is a larger freelance market for fillers, they are easier to place.
- They don't usually require a query letter because you can submit a completed manuscript in the initial contact.
- Usually crafted from personal experience or observation, they require little, if any, research.
- They can help you establish credits more quickly.
- They call attention to your writing and may open a market's door to assigned projects.
- They offer a change of pace, particularly if you're working on feature articles or a book project.
- They are an ideal vehicle for breaking into the general markets.
- They help pay for postage and paper for longer pieces.

Editors Like Fillers Because...

- Readers like short pieces that can be read quickly during a wait in a doctor's office or while on a coffee break.
- They can be read and evaluated quickly.
- They can fill odd half- or quarter-page spots.
- They can complement or supplement a longer piece on a related topic, as in the case of a sidebar.
- They discover writers who can write tightly and concisely.
- They find writers suitable for other projects.

Where to Find Material

Where do I get ideas for my fillers? Everywhere. Anywhere. Everyday. Any day. Sounds simplistic? It is. A sensitive spirit can find seeds for thought and expression wherever he looks, listens, smells, tastes, feels, and touches. I've found filler material in the memory of a first date, in the words of a talk show guest, and in the flight of a young bird. Subjects for shorts and fillers are seen through the eyes of pain, joy, grief, victory, loss, fear, faith—any and all emotions.

Ideas can sprout and be harvested from our everyday lives and living. Here's a look at some of the garden centers that carry seeds for fillers.

Personal Experiences

Examine your personal situation for ideas. If you don't already keep a journal, writer's notebook, or a file for ideas, now is the time to start one. Begin by answering a few questions. What is the composition of your family? Are you single, married, widowed, or divorced? Do you have preschoolers, teenagers, married children, grandchildren, or handicapped children? These are some general questions to get you started, but don't stop there. Dig deep into the specifics of your situation.

Here's an exercise to prepare your writing soil for fillers. At the top of a blank sheet of paper, make a column for each of the categories you come up with. For instance, a column for married, a column for a handicapped child, a column for widowed, a column for grandchildren, a column for aging parents, etc. Next, brainstorm experiences for each category and list them in the appropriate column.

Examining the elements in your life can provide you with ideas and markets for your writing.

Relationships

Think about the people in your life—parents, siblings, children, grandparents, neighbors, co-workers, and friends (past and present). You might include in your column exercise their life-situations, strengths, struggles, and any memorable interactions you've had with them. Do you have parents, in-laws, grown children, friends, or co-workers who are facing or have overcome challenges?

Several periodicals published my 500-word piece, "Fishing for Quality Time," about a truth I learned during a family fishing trip.

Knowledge

What subjects do you know about? What is your profession? What other jobs have you held? How about volunteer positions? Degrees? Areas of study? Special training? What are your hobbies and your activities? What ministries are you involved in?

Again, the column and list exercise can germinate ideas for fillers and suggest possible markets. Because I know about certain aspects of writing for publication, I've written dozens of poems and shorts for writers' publications. As a mother, I've written shorts on the parent/child relationship.

Conversations

Listen to people. Hearing about your child's day at school, your wife's workday, or your friend's problem can provide you with material, or at least an idea for a topic you can pursue.

Go where people are and eavesdrop, ever so subtly. Note, at least mentally, what people say. What are their concerns? What needs can you address? What questions can you explore in a short article, devotional, cartoon, or other filler format?

Observations

Be a people watcher. Airports, malls, restaurants, parks, the beauty shop, and the zoo are great places to observe people. Topic ideas can come from your own life or out of the lives of those around you.

Notice, even scrutinize, your surroundings. Personally, I enjoy observing critters as well as people and use those observations in devotions, articles, and poems. Plants, the night sky, inchworms—they all might serve as anecdote or illustration material.

Media

A newspaper headline, magazine article, or advertisement; a newscast, a radio program, or commercial; or a talk show or situation comedy can plant or water existing ideas for fillers.

A discussion on a talk show prompted my short magazine article, "AIDS: How Do We Respond?" published in several periodicals.

Ideas for fillers are everywhere. Like pollen, they float in the air we breath.

Trap Ideas

I have lost ideas in the winds of forgetfulness. Don't let your ideas flit by without an opportunity to root. Capture them on paper, a tape or digital recorder, or a keypad. Once you've recorded your ideas, don't throw any of them away. Though the conditions for growth may not be right at the moment, things change. Ideas mingle and plant new images.

Folders labeled "Poetry Ideas," "Devotional Ideas," "Article Ideas," "Puzzle Ideas," and so on hold slips of paper containing my seeds for titles, themes, lines, images, descriptions, phrases, and feelings. While waiting for spring, they take refuge in one of my greenhouse files. Eventually, many find fertile soil and sprout into fillers.

Find a retaining system that works for you and use it to store and organize your ideas from experiences, relationships, knowledge, conversations, and observations.

Popular Filler Formats

As I mentioned earlier there are several types of fillers. Here's a look at some tips for writing in the most commonly published categories.

Daily Devotionals

Devotionals provide spiritual nourishment for people on the run. Basically it's a short inspirational look at a verse or passage of Scripture as it pertains to everyday life. The average daily devotional is 200 to 300 words. Some publications prefer fewer words. Some accept longer pieces. Before submitting your manuscripts, check a publication's writers' guidelines for the preferred length and format.

Usually there's a Bible text or passage to read, as well as a short prayer or prayer suggestion. Sometimes there's also a thought for the day.

Financially speaking, writing daily devotionals does not provide a living, but there are countless dividends and far-reaching results. The average payment is fifteen to twenty-five dollars per devotional. Sometimes a publication only offers a byline.

Daily devotionals usually reach more people than books do. The average printing on a first book by an unknown author is ten to fifteen thousand copies (and a sell-out of those copies would be considered good sales). But your devotional in *The Upper Room* reaches millions of people, in more than forty different languages.

Devotionals allow the Holy Spirit to work through a writer's individuality. They afford an outlet for personal insights and creative expression. Devotionals can provide hope, encouragement, and an invitation for salvation to a world needing a timely word. Plus, they require the writer to have a disciplined Bible study and dynamic prayer life.

Here are a few more tips to consider and remember as you write daily devotionals:

1. Love the Word and the God of the Word.

Spending time in the Bible will result in intimacy with God and with your readers. Are you developing a close relationship with the Lord?

The late Catherine Marshall was once asked, "What advice would you give people seeking to be more creative?"

"That's easy," she answered. "I would tell them to stay intimately attuned to God."

The characteristics of our personality—thinking, acting, feeling—sharpen as we communicate with God. Personal Bible study and time in prayer are vital if we want to minister to people's needs.

2. Share Your Humanity with Your Readers.

Allow yourself to be the one who learns the lesson. Risk vulnerability by revealing a personal fault or frailty. Then show how Scripture helped you change. We learn best by example, not with a literary finger pointed at us.

3. Show Your Message Through Analogy, Anecdote, or Illustration.

An anecdote with which readers can identify is an excellent way to present biblical truth without sounding didactic or preachy. Good devotional writing is full of examples, stories, symbols, images, metaphors, and parables.

Devotionals are not mini-sermons. Avoid using demanding words such as must, should, or ought. Offer hope for a spiritually richer life through anecdotes and illustrations.

4. Select a Single Theme per Devotion.

When I first began writing, my teacher often pointed out several devotionals within each manuscript. While a Bible passage or verse may contain several topics, choose only one per meditation and maintain a tight focus. Write a theme sentence for each devotion. Ask yourself, "What is the one message or truth I want to convey?"

5. Keep a Spiritual Journal.

Read your Bible and listen to sermons with a pen in hand. Always keep a tablet or notebook nearby. Record your insights from personal Bible study, sermons, or discussions on the Bible. Jot down your ideas before they flee. I keep a file of Bible study and sermon notes. Going through old outlines allows me to make connections with personal experiences.

6. Make Withdrawals from Your Memory Bank.

You are rich in personal experiences. Look for a personal experience with a spiritual and scriptural parallel. What did God show you in that experience? How did He bring you through it?

7. Keep Terminology Specific and Easy to Understand.

Avoid theological jargon or vagueness. Not everyone understands such words as justification, propitiation, salvation, grace, or sanctification. Be as clear and precise as you can. Draw on examples to explain spiritual truths.

Use an informal, personal style. Write as if you're visiting with a friend. I like to picture a particular friend, family member, or neighbor as I write.

8. Handle Scripture Accurately.

When quoting the Bible, be exact. Include proper references and don't take verses or passages out of context. Note the Bible version you use and be aware that some publishers require use of one particular version only. Others may have no preference.

9. Make Each Word Count.

Remember, meditations are short and have specific space limitations. Devotional readers want to invest about five minutes in an inspirational jump-start for their day. Eliminate unnecessary verbiage.

When you can, replace adverbs and adjectives with active verbs and descriptive nouns. Instead of saying, "The ball was hit by Emily," say, "Emily smacked the ball." You might change "I walked slowly" to "I shuffled" or "I crept." Write tightly. Write using specific and active verbs.

10. Read and Study Lots of Daily Devotionals.

If you want to write daily devotionals, read lots of daily devotionals. But don't just read them, study them.

Look at the titles. Make, at least, a mental note of the Bible passages used. Consider the leads—the opening lines and paragraphs. Notice the style or format used. Examine the transitions from the anecdotes to illustrations of the spiritual application.

11. Research Markets Carefully.

Study the publication. Before putting your devotional in the mail, examine the writers' guidelines. These can be obtained through a publisher's Web site or by sending a self-addressed, stamped envelope to the publisher with your request. Adhere to the specific length and format needs.

Most devotional publishers don't want controversial issues addressed. Nor do they want criticism expressed in their meditations.

As a beginner, you'll submit only to the devotional markets that accept freelance submissions. Because many Christians have the misconception that writing meditations or devotionals is something anyone can do in his or her spare time, editors have been bombarded with unprofessional manuscripts. Consequently, most of the daily devotional publishers work with "assigned writers" only.

In other words, many of the publishers require submission of sample devotionals based on an assigned Scripture passage and theme. The writer has a deadline and is given an opportunity to establish credibility.

12. Consider Denominational Taboos.

Know the denomination for which you intend to write. Does your meditation adhere to a particular publication's denominational doctrine and practices?

Note that some denominational markets only accept manuscripts from writers active in one of their churches.

Book Reviews

I wrote my first book reviews in response to an advertisement I saw in *The Christian Communicator.* The editor asked for reviews of books for writers and speakers. This was a great place for me to start because those books are of special interest to me.

The purpose of book reviews is simple: you want to familiarize others with the book's contents to interest them in reading it.

Some reviews are staff-written, but many editors look for good reviewers who work as freelancers. Ask your librarian to show you where to find book reviews. Study them. Scour magazines and newspapers for them. Write for guidelines from those publications printing reviews.

If you like reading books, you might try writing book reviews. Remember to write your unbiased views concisely.

Columns

Does the average one-to-three-year wait required to see your byline in magazines have you down? Do you long to know, first-hand, that someone is reading your articles? Consider writing for your local newspaper.

Writing a regular column for the newspaper gave me immediate publication, recognition, and feedback. Perhaps you would like to be a columnist but you're wondering where to start.

First, take a few moments and make a list of subjects you know a great deal about. In the pages of newspapers and magazines you'll find columns on such topics as travel, health, gardening, psychology, computers, cooking, crafts, sports, politics, home decorating, hunting, pet care, and parenting. I'm sure you can list many more subjects. Which topics interest you the most?

Homework is important for the writer who would enter into a career as a columnist. Study your local newspaper or the magazine you wish to write for. What are its special interest columns? Take a look at your list of subjects.

Which of those may be best suited to meet the needs of your local community and, thus, the newspaper? Or, if your target is a magazine, which ones might meet the needs of that magazine? Can you sustain your topic, coming up with enough information and subtopics to keep it fresh?

Next, write some sample columns. As a general rule, keep the length close to 500 to 700 words and, certainly, under 1,000 words. As you prepare your samples, you will discover the format that best suits you and your topic.

One columnist I know writes an informational column, so she uses a formal essay style with personal anecdotes included. I wrote my newspaper columns in a chatty, personal style. Other columnists, like Ann Landers, use a question and answer format. Perhaps, like William F. Buckley, yours will be an opinion narrative, or a humorous narrative like Dave Barry's columns.

Consider, too, how often you'd like to be published. Decide how much time you can invest in preparing a column. Does your topic lend itself to a daily, weekly, or monthly printing? Most magazines print monthly, bimonthly, or quarterly. The longevity of an idea determines the frequency of the column. Many editors want a commitment of at least a year before they'll agree to run your column.

After you've polished some sample columns, you'll prepare a proposal packet for the editor. Include a proposal letter, four to six sample columns, and a self-addressed, stamped envelope.

The proposal letter is your one-to-two-page sales pitch. Make it good. Include the following information:

- Subject and slant of your column.
- A suggested title. Make it catchy.
- Your writing credits and any credentials or experience pertaining to your subject matter.
- Market statement. Tell which readers would be interested in your column and why.
- You may want to include additional column ideas to let the editor know that you can generate topics easily.
- Specify your intention to follow up with a phone call to discuss your proposal. Indicate a specific week (allow two or three weeks) when you'll get back to the editor if you haven't received a response. Follow-up is important. A follow-up call should be short and courteous. Identify yourself, refer to your proposal, and ask, "Is this a convenient time for you to discuss it?" If so, ask if he is interested or make an appointment to talk in person. If the editor is not interested, don't be discouraged. Try another newspaper or magazine.

When the answer is "Yes, let's give it a try," once you're done jumping up and down for joy, you need to ask some questions:

- How often will the column appear? How much lead time does the editor want (the time between your submission of the article and his printing it)?
- What rights will the publication buy? Usually newspapers are not copyrighted, so anything in them is in the public domain. Magazines are a different story. Know what rights they're buying.
- Ask about payment. Be prepared for the fact that some newspaper editors don't pay their columnists at all—at least, not in the beginning. However, the freelancer usually gets paid by the column inch in the newspaper business. The average compensation is from ten to fifty dollars per column for the beginner.

Granted, writing a column for a local newspaper may not pay as well as you'd like, but it will provide several benefits.

You'll receive a lot of writing experience and a great deal of exposure from your byline. You'll gain experience in meeting deadlines. Your articles will receive individual editing. Your column will help establish your reputation as a writer. You'll begin to gather a group of columns that may later be developed into a book.

Once the questions are answered and you have an agreement with the editor, write! Do your best. Writing for a local paper is an education you may get paid for.

Interested? Give it a try.

Where to Find Markets

Like ideas, markets for fillers abound anywhere and everywhere. You'll see a variety of formats for fillers in family magazines, newsletters, newspapers, trade magazines, children's magazines, state and regional magazines, community magazines, women's magazines, Sunday school or church take-home papers, denominational magazines—just about in anything you read.

The Lord's Prayer adds up to less than 100 words. Lincoln's *Gettysburg Address* can be recited in under two minutes. The *Declaration of Independence,* including the signatures, fits onto one page. Good things can be written using few words.

Pull out those idea column exercises and explore the possibilities.

Writing Picture Books for Children

6

by Christine Harder Tangvald

Good writers are those who keep the language efficient. That is to say: keep it accurate, keep it clear.

—Ezra Pound

Writing picture books involves two of my favorite things: The best AUDIENCE in the whole wide world—CHILDREN—and the best TOPIC in the whole wide world—GOD!

Those of us who write picture books have the opportunity to present our enthusiasm and passion for God in the homes and hearts of *thousands* and *thousands* of children through one of the most exciting mediums ever invented in the history of communications: picture books.

In this chapter, we'll delve into the nitty-gritty specifics of how to write and format a picture book. We'll go through several basics, such as age groups, word counts, and types of picture books. We'll cover structure and formatting. Then on to the fun stuff—special features and what I call the "Pizazz Factor." Then, we will deal with marketing.

My goal is to serve you by sharing what I've learned along the way. If I help you express your passion for Jesus with His delightful children, then this endeavor will be a success.

Remember, the words and techniques presented here are not carved in stone. This is simply *what works for me*. I cannot possibly cover every aspect of writing picture books in one chapter, so I encourage you to learn this skill from as many sources as possible.

Like, Know, and Respect: Three Essentials

1. Like

First and foremost, do you like children?

Please, only write for children if you *truly like* them. Do you find children fascinating and delightful? Do you seek out their company and spend hours with them? Do you play, visit, laugh, cry, pretend, read, color, and pray with them?

2. Know

Do you *know* today's children—what they think and what they like? Do you know the "now" world they live in and deal with every day? Do you see and interact with children on a regular basis? Do you know and understand their contemporary games, their contemporary problems, their contemporary schedules, and their contemporary goals?

Many aspects of childhood are universal—curiosity, empathy, energy, delight in discovery, etc. However, in order to write for today's children, you must know them and the world they live in TODAY!

3. Respect

Do you respect children—especially the age group you want to write for? Can you understand and feel their problems and joys in your heart? What about a skinned knee, a race won or lost, delight and amazement for a ladybug? Are these experiences important to you? They are to the child.

Respect is *vital*, because it becomes a matter of *attitude*, and that attitude will show in your writing.

Again, do you truly like, know, and respect today's child?

I have a philosophy I call "Writing on My Knees." By this, I mean two things:

1. Try to write "on your knees" at eye level with the child. This shows respect. Don't write down to the child. This not only applies to attitude, but also to topic and writing style. Is the topic age appropriate? Is the writing style age appropriate?

   Too often I have seen manuscripts at writers' conferences that are actually sermons poorly veiled as stories. Do not do this. Write to or with the child, at eye level, which places you on your knees.
2. Also, always try to write on your knees under the authority of God. Sometimes we get so excited about the topic, the method, the layout, or the concept for a book that we forget to consult God about what *He* wants.

Let's list a few general rules for writing picture books. We will discuss types of picture books, age groups, word counts, and the basic structure of fiction and nonfiction.

Types of Picture Books

Here is a list of some types of picture books:

Fiction

Contemporary
Historical
Biblical
Fantasy/allegory
Mystery
Action/adventure
Talking animal

Nonfiction	Examples:
Topical	Body, creation, holidays
Inspirational	Devotions, prayer
Informational	Children of the Bible
Concept books	Colors, shapes, counting

Biography	Moses, Martin Luther King
Novelty	
Poetry	
Picture identification	
Wordbooks	
Wordless books	
Puzzle/activity books	
Easy reader (1,000 to 1,500 words)	
Participation books (Reader involvement, Q/A)	

It is much easier to focus your theme and text if you have decided what type of book you are writing. Check out picture books at the library to see the different types. Read through fifty picture books (one hundred is better). The best way to learn how to write is to read lots of picture books. The best advice I can give you is to read and analyze the type of books you want to write: storybook, concept book, devotions, etc.

Analyze by asking questions: What type of book is this? How long is it? How many pages does it have? Is it done in single pages or spreads? Is it age appropriate in topic? Is it age appropriate in writing style? Why? Why not?

General Age Groups

Most widely used:	Sometimes used:
0-3	4-7
2-4	5-8
3-5	
- - - - - - - - - - "reading gap" (when the child begins to read)	
6-8	
8-10, 12	

Each publishing house has its own specific age group designations. Send a self-addressed, stamped envelope (SASE) and ask for a copy of its writers' guidelines or check its Web site. This will tell you exactly what each house is looking for.

Also, go to a Christian bookstore and see how the picture books are grouped by age. A bookstore is the best research library there is for a picture book writer. I try to spend one day a month browsing bookstores.

Word Count

The general rule for picture books is 200 to 1,000 words. Most picture books set the limit around 1,000 words of text. Some go up to 1,200 to 1,500 words. Anything over that moves the format up to 48 pages (discussed later), which becomes extremely expensive to produce due to the high cost of illustration. Remember, the more words, the smaller the type has to be, and the less space there is for pictures. So, *cut, cut, cut!*

Many of the strongest texts are under 500 words, but they must be 500 DYNAMITE WORDS! This will become clear as you begin to read and analyze a stack of picture books.

Structure of Fiction and Nonfiction

Fiction and nonfiction have very different structures. In the short scope of this chapter, I can only begin to touch on the important elements. I recommend you read several how-to-write books on fiction and nonfiction. You can probably find several at your local library. Also, join the Writer's Digest Book Club and start your own library of how-to-write books.

Fiction

Fiction is written on a timeline. Your story is about a piece of *time* out of your main character's life. In a picture book, it is a *short* timeline. Your story needs a beginning, a middle, and an end. Begin at a point of drama or action where something is happening. End at a point of closure, but keep things moving in between.

Fiction needs three things:

- One main character
- An interesting setting
- One dominant problem or conflict for your main character to solve. (This is where most beginning writers fail. There isn't enough conflict to sustain a strong storyline.)

Plot is what happens on your timeline—the action points that carry your story from beginning to end as your character struggles to resolve the conflict.

Theme is what your story is about. Every piece of good fiction has one dominant, well-defined, underlying universal theme: courage, perseverance, faithfulness, wisdom, etc. (For example, the theme of Peter Rabbit is disobedience.) Know your theme, focus it, and use it to intensify the drama and dynamics of your story.

In a picture book, all this (and much more) must be done in less than 1,000 words. That makes writing picture books hard work. Novelists have tens of thousands of words to develop characters, to create settings, and to set up and resolve conflicts. Try doing all this in 325 words! Every single word must count.

Nonfiction

Nonfiction is about a topic, not a timeline. It, too, has three parts:

1. An introduction
2. A body
3. A conclusion

Tightly focus your topic. Tightly focus your theme. When you are ready to begin your picture book, write a theme sentence and give the purpose of your book. Then divide your topic into sections. This becomes the body of your book. Begin with a strong, dynamic introduction. End with a summary and a conclusion that has punch. It usually restates the theme sentence. Do not allow anything in your final text that doesn't deal with your theme. Focus, and cut, cut, cut.

Do this in less than 1,000 words. Now, rewrite and rewrite. Actually, I *love* writing nonfiction. It is much easier than fiction. Also, nonfiction sells very well. (All but six of my books are nonfiction.)

Formatting

This is the topic most often left out of instructions to picture book writers. The reason is because it's easier to *show* you how this is done than it is to *tell* you how it is done.

Paper comes out of printing presses in specific page numbers—in increments of eight. It goes: 16, 24, 32, 48, 64... pages. Most picture books are published in a 24- or 32-page format. (Color books, activity books, and church resource books are usually in 32-, 48-, or 64-page format.) We will use 24- and 32-page formats.

First you subtract "front and back matter." This is the term used to describe the title page, the copyright page, and any other pages lost to gluing onto covers, etc.

We will "work" with a 24-page paperback book. We will lose only the title page and copyright page. 24 pages minus 2 pages = 22 pages left to use.

Here is the rule of thumb: 24-page formats usually have 20-22 pages of text. 32-page formats usually have 26-28 pages of text.

Now we need to define a very important word: SPREAD. Picture books are formatted in single pages and in spreads. A spread is simply the unit of space consisting of both the left page and the right page in a book. The two pages are considered one unit. We will use the term "spread" a lot in this chapter.

Many picture books are written in single pages with one piece of text and a picture on each page. Thus, in a 24-page format, you might have 22 "pieces" of story with 22 pictures. (24 pages, minus title page, minus copyright page, equals 22 pages of space to work with.)

Some picture books are written in spreads—one piece of text and one picture for 2 pages (left and right pages treated as one unit). For a 24-page format (remember, only 22 pages of space are available) you might have:

1 an introductory right page	1 page
10 10 spreads	20 pages
1 an ending left page	1 page
12 pieces of text	22 pages

This book would require 12 pieces of text. This format works very well for poetry and nonfiction.

Many picture books mix using single pages and full spreads, giving some flexibility to the author. You can choose whether you want to divide your story or topic into single pages, spreads, or to mix the two.

It is important to know that a picture book is a marriage between text and art. You don't do your own illustrations unless you are a professional artist who can fit in with a publishing house's style. The publishing company chooses the designer and illustrator. Both text and art become a vital part of the book. They work together to produce visual as well as emotional, informational, or inspirational impact.

So, picture books need art concepts—something to illustrate for every page or spread. A picture book cannot have a static text because there would be nothing to illustrate. The text must be written to evoke a new visual concept or picture every time the child turns the page. It needs a change in setting, a new action, a new or altered concept (shape, color)— something visual to illustrate that is *different* from the page or spread before and the page or spread that follows.

Christine's Magic Recipe Card Method of Layout

Once I have my story or nonfiction text outlined or written, I literally lay it out on the floor and cut it into chunks, using sheets of typing paper or large recipe cards—one sheet or card for each page or spread.

Then I read my text out loud over and over as I walk across the room. This helps me in many ways:

1. It forces me to divide the text into equal "pieces," not necessarily equal amounts of words, but equal pieces of impact. One page might only say, "BOOM!" but it might "weigh" more than a page covered with text.
2. It shows me immediately if I need to add or subtract a concept or a scene to fit into the required number of pages. Can I divide a scene into two spreads if my story is too short? Can I condense a scene into a single page if my story is too long? Should I mix and match single pages and spreads?
3. It helps me pace the text. I don't want all the impact at the beginning or ending of the book, so I check for that here. Is there enough action and drama to lead the reader through the book to the end, or is the pace flat and dead? Does my opening grab the reader? Does my ending have closure?
4. It helps me check for illustration concepts. Is there something different to illustrate on every page? Identify it.

5. This is a great time to check for pizazz. (See "The Pizazz Factor" on the following pages.) Are my characters boring? Can I put in a crescendo/decrescendo of intensity, noise, suspense, surprise? Can I add rhythm, alliteration, or an onomatopoeia word? Can I put something into dialogue to bring my characters into the immediate, right now, alive tense?

Thumbnail Sketch

Now, I coordinate the pages I have developed on my recipe cards or sheets of typing paper with the thumbnail sketch (see illustration on next page). This thumbnail sketch was given to me by an editor and has been one of the most helpful devices I have ever had in formatting a picture book. You can see all at once exactly how your book will lay out. Once I have the layout done, I actually send in a copy of this thumbnail sketch with my manuscript to the editor so she can see how I envision it.

Dummy

At this point, you can also make what is called a dummy—a simple mock-up of your book. It's easy and can be very useful. A dummy works especially well if you have incorporated a novelty feature.

For a 24-page dummy, simply fold twelve sheets of typing paper in half. Mark off your front and back matter and indicate where and how you would place your text on the pages. For a 32-page format, use sixteen sheets of paper.

A dummy provides a real feel for the flow of your book. It's fun to hold something concrete in your hands at this point.

The Pizazz Factor!

In Christian writing, we have the most exciting topic there ever was to write about: GOD. God is not dull, and God is not boring. Neither should books or stories about God be dull or boring. In fact, I think it is a sin to bore a child when you write about God.

Good Christian writing for children goes beyond simply stating facts, or simplistic moralization, and moves into the realm of *excellence*. Anything less will not do!

I think every picture book needs to contain some kind of energy, passion, or personality. Otherwise why write it? I call it PIZAZZ!

Spreads for a 24-page Picture Book

24	Copyright Page 1
Title Page 2	Begin Here 3
4	5
6	7
8	9
10	11
12	13
14	15
16	17
18	19
20	21
22	23

How do you write with pizazz? For me, it means *rewrite, rewrite, rewrite*! I often rewrite my picture books thirty to forty times.

I have developed what I call a Pizazz Factor Checklist.

Pizazz Factor Checklist

In fiction, check every page for:

Action
Drama
Emotion
Tension
Scene development
Character
Dialogue
Detail
Pace

In nonfiction, check every page for:

Focused topic
Theme
Balance
Enthusiasm
Accuracy
Structure
Understandability
Excitement
Curiosity

In both fiction and nonfiction, check every page for:

The five senses: touch, taste, smell, sight, sound
Alliteration
Active verbs
Humor
Onomatopoeia words
Specific nouns
Repetition
Rhyme
Rhythm
Suspense/mystery

Surprise
Flow
Discovery
Personalization
Contrast
Age interest
Accuracy/research
Structure
Unity of theme
Unity of format
Anticipation
Question
Goals
Simplicity

I check every sentence of every manuscript against this list before it leaves my house. As you read children's materials, analyze what methods and techniques the author used to add pizazz. Start files. Study them. Use them.

Here are a few of the most important things I check for:

1. Structure

I check the structure of my book thoroughly. This sounds simple, but it's not. It's a lot of work.

2. Verbs

I circle every verb in my picture book. An editor did this to one of my picture book manuscripts at a writers' conference, and I had more than fifteen weak verbs on one page. I was embarrassed. Now I am aware of every verb I use. I choose them carefully. If I use a "were" or a "was," I *know* it, and I know *why* I used it. If I need to use them (and often I do), I try to offset the fact with some other technique of personality or pizazz.

3. Action, Pace, Tone, Intensity, Emotion.

I check to see if anything is happening. What? Why? Can the reader feel anything? What? Why? How can I keep the child not just interested, but *fascinated* until the end of the book? Can I add suspense, tension, an element of surprise, contrast, pathos, etc. I check for opportunities for each one of these on every page of my manuscript.

4. Drama.

Is there anything to "act out" in this book? Or to feel sad about? To get excited about? Or is the text written in a flat-line, monotone style? Should I increase (or decrease) the dramatic tension? How? Where? This leads me to one of my favorite tests. I call it "The Mirror Test"!

I actually read my piece out loud, looking into a mirror. My kids think it's a riot! "Oh, it's just Mom again, in the bathroom, reading into the mirror!" But it works. Do I find myself making eye contact in the mirror as I read or gesture? Can I use voice inflection? Emotion? Where are the "act out" parts? Am I actually acting them out? Do they work? Why? Why not? Do I look surprised? Do I look sad? Do I look mad? Do I look just plain bored?

If I start to fix my hair during a certain segment, then I know I am in big trouble, and I rewrite it!

Another technique I use to manipulate the dramatic tension is the *crescendo-decrescendo* technique. Accelerate and then decelerate one or more of the following: action, tension, struggle, pace, noise, emotion, and intensity.

5. Spacing.

Sometimes the simple use of creative spacing of the text is enough to add interest to your book. I hate block typing so I avoid it. I use indents, creative repetition, lists, spaces between sections, subheadings, "personality" words, quotations, the method of predictability, and any other special feature I can think of to vary the placement of the text on the page.

6. Special Features.

Special features help sell books. Can you add a color book picture, stickers, a fun-to-do activity? How about a tear-out poster, a bookmark, or a paper doll?

One of my series of picture books is based on the special feature of personalization. (Jesus is FOR ME! The Bible is FOR ME!) One series is based on the method of predictability, the careful use of repetition of a key sentence or phrase. Another series uses the special feature of *rebus*—little pictures are included right in the text. All these are special features that add interest and uniqueness (pizazz!) to the picture book. Start collecting a file of special features that you can use in your writing.

I'm not advocating you use all of these pizazz factors in one story. That would be overkill. If only one technique applies to your writing and brings it one step closer to excellence for the Lord, then all the time and effort are worth it.

Let's take this chapter you are reading right now as an example. What one technique have I wrapped it around? I am writing it in what I call the "Conversational Mode." It didn't just happen. I selected it on purpose.

I feel I am talking directly with you. I have "you" pictured here sitting in my living room with me, and we are chatting about writing picture books. Hopefully, it is more interesting to read than an unimaginative repetition of straight facts.

Go for it and have some fun!

A Short Section on Marketing

Send a complete manuscript of your picture book typed in professional manuscript format. I coordinate page divisions of the text on my manuscript to match the page numbers on the thumbnail sketch. These are indicated in the left margin of the manuscript.

Do I send a book proposal? Yes, always. To me, a proposal is a sales piece. It is an advertisement for your book. At present, your book is unemployed. The manuscript, together with your proposal, is your book's job application. The proposal answers the what, how, why, and who of your book.

What makes your book so special that it stands out from the rest? Does it? If not, rewrite it until it does.

My motto is: "Tell Them! Sell Them!" Be convincing and professional, but *never* be pushy! However, if you aren't really excited about your book, why should the editor be? Often, after I have written my proposal, I have to go back and rewrite my book until it can live up to the glowing sales piece I created for it. I try never to send in a picture book manuscript that is weaker than my proposal promises.

Things to Include in a Book Proposal

- Dynamite proposal statement
- Purpose statement
- Title
- Theme
- Length
- Format
- Special features or methods used
- Goals
- Market analysis—why this book is needed and an analysis of the competition
- Short plan on how to expand it into a series, if possible, including titles, themes, one-paragraph plots
- Anything else relevant to this particular project

I always include a flexibility statement to show I am willing to rewrite it into whatever format might fit their current need.

I type the proposal in single-spaced, nonfiction format. I set my subheads in all caps, and I triple space between topics. My proposals are usually between one and four pages long.

Always include a cover or query letter. A cover letter is your introduction to an editor. It is your handshake. Write it well. It tells a lot about your writing skill.

Start with a grabber introduction. Include a short, enticing summary of your project. Tell a little about your qualifications, or refer to an enclosed "Author Information Sheet." Indicate the inclusion of your proposal. Thank the editor for his consideration.

To me, a cover letter is a "hook" to:

- Show the editor you can write well.
- Entice the editor to read your proposal.

All this is done in less than one page.

My goal is: By the time the editor has scanned my cover letter and browsed through my proposal, he is so impressed with my project, my topic, my professionalism, and my writing that he can't wait to read the manuscript.

My picture book package:

- Cover letter
- Proposal
- Thumbnail Sketch
- Manuscript
- SASE

Now *write* a picture book, polish it, finish it, type it, and put it in the mail! Then, write two more picture books while you wait for the rejection slip! (I had nineteen rejections before I sold my first piece for $3.) Writing picture books is hard work, but it's worth it.

Remember, when God sent us a *Savior,* He didn't send us a rough outline or a first draft. He didn't send a fourth draft, or a tenth or twentieth draft. He didn't send something that was just "pretty good." He didn't send something that was "almost right."

God sent us "His Very Best." He sent His only Son. So, we should send Him our very best.

I encourage you to read and reread, write and rewrite your manuscripts until they sparkle and shine—until you would be proud and excited to read them to Jesus Himself. It's my feeling that when one of our books is read to a single child that is exactly what happens.

I hope this chapter will help in some small way to enable you to express your passion for our Lord through the exciting medium of picture books. I wish for you God's richest blessings as you strive to bring the glorious "Good News" to His precious children.

Writing First Chapter Books and Junior Novels

7

by Gayle G. Roper

I try to write on my knees under the authority of God and at eye level with the child.

—Christine Harder Tangvald

Picture a movie set, actors in place, crew in position, waiting. Suddenly the director yells,"Action!" and the scene unfolds.

The key to writing for—and being read by—children is found in the director's single word: ACTION!

Kids are physical; kids are doers. If and when they ponder the great issues of life, it's in a linear, straight-to-the-point fashion.

"Will Fido go to heaven when he dies?"

"Where do babies come from?"

"If heat rises, why is the snow on the top of the mountains?"

"Does God have hands?"

The most direct answer an adult can think of is the best to give a child. In kids' fiction, the more action a writer can devise the better. Obviously the action is all carefully focused and ordered, but the story always moves forward.

Hard on the heels of *action* comes the imperative that kids' fiction is written "To kids, For kids, and About kids."

There have been some outstanding books in which kids are the viewpoint characters, but these books were written for adults. Harper Lee's *To Kill a Mockingbird* has an eleven-year-old viewpoint character named Scouting, but it is not a book to, for, or about kids. Another example is Olive Ann Burns's wonderful *Cold Sassy Tree* in which a fourteen-year-old boy, Will Tweedy, is the viewpoint character. However the themes and their application are definitely adult.

To Kids, For Kids, and About Kids

One of the easiest traps to fall into in writing kids' fiction is placing the adults too much in the forefront—not intentionally like the above mentioned writers, but because in real life adults are in the forefront of kids' lives.

Adults buy kids' food and clothes and provide their housing. Adults take them places, interesting ones like Disney World and necessary ones like the doctor's office. Adults tell them they must be in bed by nine, must go to school and church, and must not play with Billy Walker because he punches people and says bad words.

Kids don't want to read about adults doing things to resolve stories. That's too much like real life. Kids want to read about kids being heroes, kids solving mysteries, and kids being the smart ones.

Suppose two kids are walking in the woods and come upon a third who is hurt. In real life, the first two would run for the nearest adult because they don't know what to do and because they're scared. The adult would call the ambulance. The adult would go to the injured kid. The adult would resolve the situation.

However, if a writer pulls an adult into a kids' story like that, the readers won't be happy. They want the two who find the hurt child to rescue him. They'll accept it if the kids call an ambulance, but they'll be much happier if the kids can fix the injury themselves. And they'll be delighted if the kids do all this while they're pursued by an evil adult or stalked by a hungry mountain lion or lost in the blizzard of the century.

I wanted to write about adoption for kids, so I decided on a junior novel that would show that putting a child up for adoption is not the worst kind of rejection. My challenge was to allow Jase, a thirteen year old struggling with his adoption, to accept this truth through circumstances and his own thought processes, not the convenient words of an adult. Jase's insight, presented lightly and succinctly so the readers won't skip over it, must flow easily and seamlessly out of and back into the story.

At the end of Jase's story (*7th Grade Soccer Star*, Chariot Books), the climactic soccer game is over, and everyone has gone home except Jase and his father. They are waiting to give a ride to Rand who is Jase's nemesis, the class hero/bully, and the son of a single mother who, once again, has gone off with a boyfriend. Here is what follows:

> I jogged to the locker room and looked in. It was quiet and dark. I had just turned to leave when I heard a loud sniff. I stopped, startled, and listened intently. More sniffs. Someone was crying.
>
> Suddenly the lockers erupted in a great rattling. Someone was beating on them.
>
> Then there was silence again.
>
> I peered carefully into the alcove where the noise was coming from. There stood Rand, head down, shoulders slumped, leaning against the lockers.
>
> Ever so quietly I tiptoed back to the main door, wondering what to do. I certainly didn't want Rand to know I'd seen him crying. He'd be so upset that I knew he'd spend the rest of his life trying to get me.
>
> *Boy*, I thought. *There are lots worse ways to reject someone than by placing him for adoption. There's everyday rejection, and that's got to be the worst.*
>
> I grabbed the door and banged it loudly against the wall. "Hey, Rand!" I yelled. "You in there?"
>
> After a small silence a surly voice answered, "You still here, shrimp?"

"Yeah. We're waiting for you."

"Be right there."

I turned and ran to the car. By the time Rand climbed into the front, I was safely seated in the back. He stared out his window all the way to his empty house.

Notice how Jase reaches his own conclusion. Notice how it flows out of and back into the action. Notice how it's TO, FOR, and ABOUT kids.

First Chapter Book

A fairly new entry on the children's publishing scene is the early reader known as a first chapter book. The name "first chapter" may come from two places. One, these little books are the first books kids read that actually have chapters. Two, the entire book is the length of the first chapter of a good-sized adult novel. Take your pick.

Beginning readers are proud of the fact they can finally read, and first chapter books are the bridge for these new readers from picture books to junior novels. First chapter books have eight to ten chapters and are 6,000 to 8,000 words long. The difficulty comes in developing well-defined characters and a complete story in such a short space. Dialogue is crucial to the success of a first chapter book, lots and lots of it. Young readers enjoy humor and mystery thrown in with their action, and I recommend a single viewpoint character to prevent confusion and promote reader identification. First person works well but is not necessary.

Junior Novels

All the qualities that make good adult fiction make good junior fiction: conflict, suspense, pacing, focused plotting, complex characters, a strong beginning, a tense middle, and a satisfying ending.

Because the characters' emotions and thoughts are more important to junior readers than to beginning readers, remembering our own struggles as kids can often give us the feel we want. How did I feel when I was the last one picked for a team? How did I react when I blew the spelling bee over a simple word I really knew or when I was yelled at for something I didn't do?

I remember when a nice but not very popular girl in my sixth grade class had a party, and hardly anyone came. I don't know why people didn't come, but I remember the hurt she felt and the distress I felt for her. I wanted to use this memory in Race to the Finish (Chariot Books) to show the increasing distress of a girl named Judy. I wrote the party much as I remembered it.

When I read the scene aloud to my husband, he said, "Okay idea, but make the party up-to-date. The kids need to play computer games or watch a video—something kids would do today."

He was right. While the emotions in my memory could transfer because the pain of a snub never changes, the specifics could not. Junior readers can spot ancient history quickly.

The Differences

Perhaps the easiest way to present the differences between first chapter books and junior novels is to show the same opening as it is appropriate for each. I will also include a short picture book text of the same story.

A Picture Book

"Don't step in that hole," said Dad. "I'll fix it tomorrow. Let's go play ball."

I hit the ball and Jake chased it. Then it was my turn in the outfield.

I heard something funny. "Listen, Jake. Do you hear that?"

Two kittens tumbled out of the tall grass.

"Oh, Daddy," said Jake, "Can we keep them?"

Andy, our collie, became the kittens' mother.

One day the kittens were lost, and Jake and I couldn't find them. Andy found them.

"Dad," I said, "how do we get them out of the hole in the floor?"

All the missing details like where the hole was, what the kittens looked like, and where Andy found them would be obvious from the illustrations.

A First Chapter Book

Chapter 1

"That's enough work for one night," said Dad. He put his saw down and closed his toolbox. "Don't step in that hole in the floor, kids."

The people who lived in our house before us had messed up the floor in my room, and Dad was fixing it.

"Come on, Scooter," said Dad to me. "Come on, Jake. Let's go play ball."

"Coming!" I grabbed my jacket and my baseball glove. I jumped into the car and landed on top of my sister Jake and her bony knees. Umph!

"Get off me, Scooter," she yelled.

"Get out from under me," I yelled back. "This is my side of the car!"

I stared at Jake, and she stared at me. Then she climbed over to her side.

"Thank you, Jake," I said politely.

She made a face at me.

Jake's real name is Jacqueline Anne. I always kid her that she goes by Jake because she can't learn how to spell Jacqueline.

Jake's one year older than me. She's nine and in third grade. I'm eight and in second grade. Most of the time, Jake is a great sister. Most of the time.

Dad pitched to me first, and I swung as hard as I could. I missed.

"That's the way to hit the air," Jake yelled.

I made believe I couldn't hear her. I knew I'd hit the next one out to her. Or the next one. Or the next one.

And I did. I even hit one over her head. I cheered as she chased it.

"Okay," called Dad. "You kids switch places."

Jake and I were running past each other when I heard something. I stopped and so did she.

"What's wrong?" she asked.

"Did you hear that?" I said. I pointed to the tall grass at the edge of the field. "Listen."

She tilted her head. "I don't hear anything."

I walked to the tall grass and got real still. So did Jake. "There it goes again," I said. "Did you hear it this time?"

Jake listened hard. "Yes," she said, excited. "I hear it! There's something in the grass!"

Notice that there is much more detail in this story than in the picture book, but there still is virtually no thought or emotion developed. All is action and dialogue.

A Junior Novel

"That's enough work for one night," said Dad. He put his saw down and closed his toolbox. "Be careful not to step in that hole in the floor."

I looked at the hole in my bedroom floor and wondered about the people who had lived here before us. How in the world had they made a hole in the floor? And why?

Did the father say, "Let's have some fun tonight, kids. We're going to have a contest to see who can make a hole in the floor first"?

Every time I got up in the night, I had to be careful where I stepped.

"Come on, Scooter," Dad said. "Let's play some ball."

I always enjoyed playing ball with Dad. Some of the guys in my sixth grade class would die before they'd play with their fathers, but I didn't mind. Dad was a very good athlete for his age.

I jumped in the car and landed on top of my sister Jake. "Oh, no!" I said. "I didn't think you were coming!"

"You don't want me along because I always beat you," she said.

Unfortunately she was right. It's incredibly embarrassing to have your thirteen-year-old sister wipe you up at the plate. "Isn't it about time you started calling yourself Jacqueline and acting like a girl instead of a tomboy?" I asked not unkindly.

I think she took special pleasure in beating me that night.

We were ready to leave when I heard a strange noise coming from the tall grass that rimmed the ball field.

"Hear that, Jake?"

She cocked her head and listened. "What is it?"

Imagine our surprise when two of the fattest, fluffiest kittens you've ever seen came tumbling out of the grass. The miniature gray lion ran right up to Jake and sat on her feet. I picked up the white one with a black patch covering his eye. I don't know how the cats felt, but for Jake and me, it was love at first sight.

Notice how we get into the mind of our viewpoint character to a much greater degree. We know what he thinks and what he feels as well as what he does and what he says.

I still remember the emotional connection I felt with the first historical novel I read in which the main character was a kid my age. I couldn't believe how much fun I had reading the book. The adventure the hero and I shared was wonderful. I knew I wanted to read books like this one forever.

We write for kids because we want our books to be the ones that make that connection, the ones that make a kid want to read forever. And if they learn something of the Lord in the process, could we ask for more?

Ten Steps in Writing a Novel

8

by Carole Gift Page

Every novel should have a beginning, a muddle, and an end. The "muddle" is the heart of your tale.

—Peter de Vries

When I wrote my first novel, *Rachel's Hope*, many years ago, I had little idea how to begin, so I simply rolled paper into my typewriter and typed, "Chapter One." After five years of rewriting, polishing, and collecting a dozen rejection slips, I finally saw my novel published. Fortunately, since then I've honed my skills and streamlined my approach to writing novels. Now, in the face of pressing deadlines, I may complete a teen novel in a matter of weeks or an adult-level novel in a few months.

Before I share with you the ten steps that take me from idea to finished manuscript, let me say a word about preparing to write. I purchase an accordion file for all my materials, including synopsis and character sketches, rough drafts, notes, research materials, correspondence, audio and video tapes, and anything else pertinent to the project.

At times, I've had up to six files in my office with works in progress. The files keep all my materials at my fingertips, travel well, and help me to "compartmentalize" each project and avoid confusion, so I don't go slightly daft trying to keep everything straight. Occasionally, when I discover I have too much material to contain in an accordion file, I buy a plastic stackable crate for the "overflow."

Now, let's get on with your novel and take those ten steps, one by one.

Step One: Begin with an Idea

Begin with an idea for a particular *theme*, a particular *plot*, or a particular *character*. Eventually all three must be woven together to create your novel. Imagine a triangle with theme as the base and plot and character making up its sides to form a satisfying story.

How do I define each of these terms?

Theme

The theme is the purpose or intent of your novel revealed as a unifying idea or premise, which, while not glaringly obvious to the reader, holds the action together as an invisible thread holds together a pearl necklace. The theme is your "take-away," the central impression you want to leave with your reader. It's always there giving organization, direction, and unity, but never calling undue attention to itself. Many writers develop their plots and characters without giving serious thought to theme, and yet the theme is what plot and characters are strung on. Proceeding without a clear-cut theme is like trying to hang out the wash without a clothesline.

I suggest you write your theme in a single sentence and tape it above your typewriter or computer as a reminder of what you're essentially trying to say. Keep in mind the difference between *theme* and *subject*. Your subject can often be said in one or two words, but your theme should be put in a complete sentence, because it's what you personally want to say about your subject. For example, your subject might be "abortion," while your theme might be stated, "Women who have abortions are also victims."

What specific theme do you wish to convey in your novel? If you begin with theme, think of characters and a plot that would best express the theme you wish to communicate.

Plot

The plot is the action of your novel. Your main character encounters a series of complications in his effort to reach a specific goal or resolve a seemingly overwhelming problem. The plot must evolve out of the needs and motivations of your main characters and must in some way be crucial to their well-being. Remember, *conflict is essential to plot!* A story without conflict is merely a series of incidents that will not likely hold your reader's interest.

If you begin with plot, ask yourself what type of characters would be most likely to be involved in such a plot and what theme might be conveyed?

Character

The character is the person (or persons) who is central to the plot and through whom the theme of the story is revealed. He or she must be depicted realistically and evoke the reader's empathy and emotion. Your main or viewpoint character should change in some recognizable way through the course of your story.

If you begin with character, consider what type of plot and theme would best demonstrate your character's traits and inner qualities.

Step Two: Write a Synopsis (Summary) of the Story to the Degree that It Has Already Occurred to You

In a synopsis, the principle is, "Tell, don't show," whereas in the novel itself the rule is, "Show, don't tell!" To begin your synopsis you don't need a finished plot in mind. Just putting down what you know so far will take you to the point where new material can flow into your mind. Using a right-brain, free-writing approach, I write my novel synopses in narrative style, third person, present tense, sometimes even adding bits of dialogue, description, or notes for future research as they occur to me.

Later, I edit a polished, shortened version of the synopsis for my publisher, but my original, unedited copy becomes my "bible" or "road map" to guide me in my writing. Here's the beginning of the seven-page synopsis of my novel, *Family Reunion* (Crossway Books):

> After a three-year absence, Justin Cahill returns to his family homestead for the death-watch of his father, who has only days to live. Justin, associate pastor of a large California church, faces his parents and younger brother Chris with a heavy heart: A burden for their salvation, guilt over choosing the ministry instead of the family furniture business, and a nagging sense of failure and self-doubt after being passed over for the position of senior pastor of his church. Even Justin's relationship with his wife and son is strained. He is too self-absorbed to be the lover and companion his wife Robyn needs, and his son Eric is intent on a career in contemporary Christian music rather than fulfilling Justin's dream of a son in the ministry.

Do you see how the synopsis *tells?* "Just the facts, ma'am," to quote a vintage detective. Let's compare this synopsis with the opening of the actual novel itself:

> Going home.
>
> Two days on the road now.
>
> Justin Cahill was traveling east on Interstate 90 with his wife Robyn and their son Eric, heading for America's heartland in their silver-blue Toyota Corolla. It was mid-December. Nearly Christmas.
>
> Heat, dry and oppressive, belched from the dashboard heater, parching Justin's throat. Too much heat, giving off a hot electric smell, repugnant, a stark, ironic contrast to the icy swirls on the windshield, belying the bitter, bone-numbing cold outside, the endless stretches of barren, ice-swept landscape.
>
> Going home.
>
> The phrase summoned images of familiar, aging faces, comfortable old rooms, crackling fires, child voices singing, "Over the river and through the woods...." Long dormant feelings blended with faint, moldering sensations—tricks of the mind. Memories sprang from shadowed crevices, from nowhere, sharp and surreal, with a stinging, swift reality, and then rebounded with the sudden snap of a slingshot.
>
> Going home.

> The radio blared, static-scratchy, not quite tuned in.
>
> Willie Nelson was singing, his voice low and gravelly, throbbing with a husky passion.

See the difference between the synopsis and the novel itself? While the synopsis summarizes or *tells*, the novel *shows*, immediately drawing the reader into an actual scene filled with lots of sensory details and description.

As you write your synopsis, you might wonder at what point you can be sure you have a well-developed plot. You have a solid, cohesive plot (whether you're writing a novel or short story) when you can answer these eleven questions:

- Who is the main character in your story?
- What is he like as a person—strengths and weaknesses?
- Who are the key people who will affect his life?
- What is your main character's major conflict?(What is he trying to accomplish or resolve, or what important lesson must he learn about himself?)
- How does he attempt to resolve the conflict?
- What obstacles does he encounter in his efforts to reach his goal?
- How does he overcome each obstacle or complication?
- What is the climax/dramatic turning point of your story?
- What is the final resolution of your story?
- What change will occur in your main character?
- Why is this story worth telling? (Have a worthy theme!)

Most of my synopses run about ten pages, double-spaced, for teen novels and from fifteen to twenty pages for adult novels, although one synopsis ended up thirty-three pages, single-spaced! Remember, a well-done synopsis will guide and reassure you through the long, lonely labor of birthing a book.

Step Three: Write Character Sketches for All Primary and Secondary Characters

How do I create fictional characters? I begin with feelings and impressions—hazy, shadowy figures in my imagination, without substance or form. I let them germinate in my mind until they take on identities and motivations. When they are ready to be named, I make lists of first and last names from phone books, baby books, or school yearbooks. When I find the right name for my character, I go through my extensive picture file looking for his or her face—a photo that matches my mental image of my character. Then, armed with name and photo, I go to my computer and, using a free-style, right-brain approach, I write an extensive character sketch, probing my character's attitudes, needs, motivations, and background.

What do I include in these case histories?

- *A character's physical appearance:* Not just whether he's tall, dark, and handsome or short, fat, and ugly. Rather, what separates him from the masses and makes him unique, one in a million?
- *His personality and temperament*: Is he cool and laid back, hot and fiery, aggressive, passive, impulsive, or cautious?
- *His motivations*: What makes him act the way he does? What are his felt, or perceived, needs? What are his real needs? What does he desire more than anything else in the world?
- *His background and family history*: History tends to repeat itself in generation after generation, as evidenced in the biblical concept of "the sins of the fathers." Beliefs and actions are deeply rooted in the past.
- *His general attitude toward others and himself*: Does he accept himself and others? Does he have identity and self-esteem problems to work through? Or does he have a healthy self-concept?
- *His outlook on life*: Is it positive? Negative? Fearful? Reckless? Practical? Romantic?
- *His habits, both good and bad*: Habits define him as a character. Does he eat a leisurely breakfast of bacon and eggs or grab a cup of black coffee on the run? Is his desk cluttered or spotless? Does he keep appointments on time or always arrive ten minutes late?
- *His education, profession, and station in life*: What does a character's career tell about him, his abilities, interests, and long-range goals? A diplomat or university professor will likely have different concerns and ways of expressing them than a taxi driver or steelworker. At the same time, be wary of stereotypes. Perhaps that diplomat got his start as a taxi driver.

- *His strengths and weaknesses*: Every human personality has both a light and dark side. A balanced mixture of these lights and darks creates a three-dimensional character, but keep in mind that some traits can be both a strength and weakness. For example, the strong, silent type who refuses to open up and communicate with his mate.
- *His idiosyncrasies*: What gestures or mannerisms are peculiar to this character? Does he pull on his ear, clear his throat, tap his fingers, fidget with his collar, lick his lips, fiddle with his glasses, twist his ring, or shrug his shoulders? (Of course, if he does all these at once, he has a real problem!)
- *His voice*: Avoid the trap of letting all your characters sound alike—like you, the author! Readers "hear" a character's voice in their heads, and they'll cringe if he doesn't sound authentic. Worse, they'll stop reading if characters don't have distinctive voices. Determine what rhythm of speech your character has—smooth, flowing sentences or short and choppy? What tone of voice—soft and mellow, deep, nasal, singsong, melodic, breathy, gravelly, or monotone? Does he mumble? Have an accent? Use big words to impress people? Stutter? Speak too loud? Too fast? Does he speak with an affectation that puts distance between himself and others or with a warmth that puts others at ease? Whatever the case, make him a one and only original!

By the time I've finished exploring the personalities of all my characters, I have a clear mental picture of how they relate to and impact one another. I also usually select five or six key words that characterize each person in my book; then I look up those words in my thesaurus or Rodale's *Synonym Finder* and list the synonyms for each word. These lists remind me of my characters' essential traits and help me keep my characters consistent throughout the story.

When I want to explore a character's feelings in depth, I mentally step into his skin and write spontaneously in first person for ten to fifteen minutes without stopping. Sometimes, what appears on the page surprises me. I marvel, wondering where the material came from. Until that moment, even I, the author, wasn't consciously aware of how that character felt. Such revelations are part of the joy and wonder of writing novels.

This instinctive, freewheeling exercise was used to "discover" Justin's memories of his brother and father in *Family Reunion*. By tapping into my own subconscious, I was able to trace raw undercurrents of emotion and unexpected complexities in Justin's relationship with his father and brother. Here's a sample, adapted into third person in the actual novel:

> He remembered his boyhood in shimmering shades of burnt orange twilights—he and Chris playing kickball out in the weed-torn field down the road, running breathless and shouting into the thin cold night air, all the boys from the neighborhood gathering around shouting back and forth, exchanging catcalls and dirty words and slapping one another around, showing off, pretending to be bold and brave and invincible....
>
> Chris was more frail than the others, ...a frightened doe-like look in his eyes, like a startled deer Justin and his dad had seen once while hunting in the woods up north—Chris's expression was like that, and it was a look that irritated Justin; sometimes he wanted to slap his brother, startle him out of that look, take away the odd, half-terrified glint that made other boys take advantage of him, made them chase him and tease him, even when he was just a string-bean eight-year-old....
>
> But perhaps there was no reason for Justin to pity Chris after all. Chris had ultimately won their father's approval, had slipped right into the mold Victor Cahill had created for his sons. Justin had refused to fit the mold, had refused to be twisted into his father's image; but Chris had been as compliant as wet clay, had slipped without protest into the role their father had created at first for Justin, and then given to Chris by default.
>
> Justin had feared his father in those days, those callow, fleeting, bumptious days of childhood—days that struck him now as not quite real, improbable, preposterous, pages from a comic book, reels from an old-time movie. Surely not his own life, not something he had actually lived.

Try this imagination-probing technique yourself. You'll be surprised by what your characters will tell you!

Step Four: Break Your Synopsis into Chapters

You may want to keep a separate file folder for each chapter, containing your rough drafts and any pertinent information or research. Usually I go through my synopsis and draw lines where I think the material can naturally divide into chapters. I also underline in red all material I want to use in my edited or abridged synopsis accompanying my proposal to a publisher.

As you divide your work into chapters, be sure something significant happens in each chapter to forward the action. Always include conflict and emotion. In a sense, each chapter has its own beginning, middle, and end, although the "end" serves more as a springboard to the next chapter. Remember, your novel should have a number of intensely dramatic moments, building like stair steps toward the highest point or climax of your story. Make certain all chapters point toward your central theme, developing and enhancing it.

Step Five: Write Descriptions of the Main Locations

Your descriptions may include foreign locales or your own hometown, historical sites, imaginary or futuristic cities, or your own living room. The point is: Do your homework. Be accurate and vivid in setting the scene, drawing from all five senses to capture your characters in their natural environment. Small but insightful details will hit home with readers, providing that ring of truth that makes your story live and breathe.

Don't trust your memory for such details. Whenever possible, go to the location where your story takes place and write out your descriptions on the spot. You may even wish to videotape or take photographs for future reference.

When Doris Elaine Fell and I coauthored the "Mist Over Morro Bay" series of mystery-romance novels, we selected a cruise ship to Alaska as the setting for our last novel, *Beyond the Windswept Sea.* We both had the opportunity to take separate Alaskan cruises for our research. I personally interviewed officers and staff, toured the ship, took pictures, and even videotaped a man-overboard drill in the icy waters of Glacier Bay. Did such research make the novel more authentic? I think so. After reading our book, a woman who had also been on an Alaskan cruise told me, "I enjoyed *your* cruise more than mine!"

Take a look at a few descriptive passages from *Beyond the Windswept Sea.* Notice how we tried to weave scenic descriptions in with our characters' ongoing actions to keep the story moving and avoid sounding like a travelogue.

> We drove around the waterfront, catching the pungent smells of pulp mills and salmon canneries, then wended our way past towering spruce, mountain ash with red berries, and barren cedar.
>
> We made our way toward Creek Street—a ragged string of rustic houses teetering on spindly pilings over a raging stream.

If you can't visit the locations in your novel, visit your public library and read about them. Don't just wing it from your armchair, trusting vague generalizations to convey a strong sense of place. Write your own detailed descriptions from photographs in travel books. Interview people who have been there. In our novel *Storm Clouds over Paradise,* Doris and I created our own island in the Caribbean by writing descriptions from travel photos. Here are random samples:

> There stood the sprawling, two-story Windy Reef Hotel, looming like a refurbished Georgian plantation, its pillars glistening white in the sunlight...surrounded by a profusion of riotous colors—full-blooming scarlet bougainvillea, exotic lavender orchids, and sweet-scented frangipani.
>
> Tamarind trees and palms weighted with ripened coconuts lined the water's edge, their fronds dipping and waving lazily in the cooling breeze.
>
> We crossed to the row of open-air booths where kilo scales dangled from makeshift burlap awnings while bulging sacks of dried beans and red peppers basked in the sun. The bins were heaping with red tomatoes, hills of onions, sliced watermelon, bruised bananas, fly-dotted mangoes, and pineapples with spiky stalks.

A final word on describing locations: Make sure your descriptions appeal to all five senses—sight, sound, smell, taste, and touch (or texture). Put your emphasis on specific descriptive nouns and verbs, and, to a lesser extent, on adjectives and adverbs.

Step Six: Do Necessary Research on All Subjects

Your objective facts must be accurate to sustain the illusion of reality and give credibility to your emotional details; thus, research is as vital for fiction as for nonfiction.

Remember, primary sources are always better than secondary sources. Don't be satisfied to simply read a book or article on your topic. Go directly to the source for information. Talk with people who've experienced what your character is experiencing. Interview police officers, lawyers, detectives, psychologists, doctors, nurses, military personnel—anyone who is willing to share his perspective and shed light on the topics covered by your novel.

For my novel *Kara*, in which a character is severely burned, I visited a burn unit and borrowed a nurse's manual offering detailed instructions for caring for burn patients. For my teen novel *Maria's Search*, I summoned my courage and went on a police ride-along through Watts, where I witnessed several drug deals occurring on street corners in broad daylight. (Only later did I panic as I recalled signing a form absolving the police of any blame in the event of my death or injury.)

While writing *Hallie's Secret* about child sexual abuse, I interviewed a psychologist, a lawyer, a woman who had been abused as a child, and foster parents and families who had adopted abused children. I read every book I could find on the subject and even attended a foster parents' seminar dealing with abuse.

You might wonder whether you as a novelist have a right to "bother" the experts for information. "Will they resent my queries or consider me intrusive or meddlesome?" No! In all my years of seeking out the experts, I've found them to be helpful, if not eager to share their expertise. And why not? Their words of wisdom may end up in the pages of a book, and let's face it, there's something about the publishing mystique that most people find irresistible. They're thrilled to contribute their knowledge for posterity.

Step Seven: Begin the Actual Writing

Frankly, at any point in these first six steps you may find yourself compelled to begin your actual novel. That's fine. When you're ready, you'll sense it. When that elusive muse nudges or inspires you, seize the opportunity to write. But don't get so caught up in the writing that you neglect your organization and research. Let your story ripen; don't pluck it when it's green. By the same token, don't let your story become overripe. That is, don't get so caught up in the preparations for your novel that you never get around to writing it!

I suggest that you write an entire chapter at a sitting, if possible. Review your synopsis, character sketches, and research materials as necessary. Then write freely, with minimal editing, visualizing your scenes and letting yourself experience your characters' emotions. Have fun with your story. See your writing as a great adventure that heightens all of your senses and makes you prickle with excitement.

What you feel as you write is what your reader will feel as he reads. If you feel you are slogging through the material and barely keeping your head above water, your reader will feel that same sense of drudgery. If you take pleasure in the writing, however, your reader will take pleasure in the reading.

Step Eight: Don't Be Afraid to Change Your Outline or Synopsis

The process of writing is a journey, an adventure, an exploration of the unknown. You may find that your novel takes new directions, the characters evolve differently from what you expected, and the plot needs to be adjusted to accommodate new ideas and revised goals. Fine. That's natural. Don't be anxious. Keep your outline as a loose structure to guide you in your writing, but be flexible enough to respond to your own creative instincts and impulses.

Think of your synopsis as a road map to guide you in your travels. Once you actually begin your journey, you may discover other side roads and avenues more exciting or suitable than the path you marked out. Remember, your synopsis is there only to serve you; don't make yourself a slave to it. Experiment with new routes as you please.

Step Nine: Write the Entire Rough Draft; Then Evaluate What You Have Written

An artist would be foolish to finish one small corner of his painting while leaving the rest of the canvas blank. By the same token, don't insist on editing your first few chapters to perfection before tackling the rest of your novel. Rather, work at completing the entire rough draft before going back for intensive editing. Why? You may find that your perspective has changed drastically and your original vision for the work has undergone a transformation. When the entire "picture" is finished, you can step back and scrutinize the whole. Give yourself—and your work—time and space. Only then can you come back fresh to analyze and evaluate the separate parts.

Ask yourself these questions:

- Have I achieved my purpose in writing this novel?
- Are my characters lifelike, interesting, sympathetic, compelling, unique, and realistically motivated?
- Do I make my reader care deeply about my main character?
- Do I have a worthy theme? An engrossing, credible plot?
- Have I utilized the tools of fiction (dialogue, description, scenes, characterization, conflict, etc.) effectively?

While you wrote your rough draft in a spontaneous, right-brain mode, now you will want to put your inner "critic" in the driver's seat for your rewrite. That's the key word. Be willing to rewrite, rewrite, and rewrite some more. Check your spelling, punctuation, grammar, clarity of expression, facts, logic, pacing, style, and tone.

If possible, when you've given it all you've got, give your manuscript to someone else to evaluate—another writer, an editor, a critique group, someone whose judgment you trust. Even the most professional writer occasionally has tunnel vision and needs the objectivity of another person. Be responsive to criticism, not defensive. Few published writers have thin skin; years of deflecting rejection slips have given most of us tough hides.

Step Ten: Submit Three Sample Chapters and Your Synopsis (Outline) to a Publisher

You may begin submitting your proposal as soon as you have several chapters completed. It's permissible to try one publisher or several, as long as you let the editors know you are querying several publishers at once. If your proposal interests them, most publishers will want to see an entire manuscript from an unpublished novelist. A novelist with several books to her credit may receive a contract on the basis of a proposal.

Regardless of your status, I suggest you begin submitting your proposal before completing your novel. It may take months to receive a reply, and in the meantime, you can continue to write. You may be fortunate enough to have your novel completed about the time you find a publisher who wants to take a look at it.

Your proposal should be as polished and error-free as you can make it. First impressions count. There is no excuse for a sloppy manuscript. Enclose a brief letter of introduction (one page, no more than two), stating your writing background and qualifications, what your novel is about, and your target audience. Most publishers want to know six things about your manuscript: subject, purpose, theme, method, importance, and market.

When mailing your proposal, put your cover letter first, followed by your synopsis, then your sample chapters (usually the first three). Don't forget to enclose a self-addressed, stamped envelope (SASE), and pray that the editor won't need it. Who knows? You may have written the "great American novel" the whole world is waiting to read!

Taking the Mystery out of Mysteries

9

by Gayle G. Roper

No tears in the writer, no tears in the reader. No surprise in the writer, no surprise in the reader.

—Robert Frost

A mystery novel is basically a highly structured novel of action based on the theme of crime and punishment. It is a wonderful genre for a Christian to write because of the automatic consideration of life and death choices and consequences.

Murder is the central crime of most mysteries because it is a deed that the reader will want punished. The taking of someone's life is the ultimate crime, the greatest possible offense. From Cain's killing of Abel until today, murder has always been and is still considered reprehensible.

The attraction of the mystery is found in the puzzle solving, and the puzzle is worth unraveling because of the enormity of the crime.

General Requirements of a Modern Mystery Novel

1. *The writer must play fair with the reader.* All information that the reader needs to solve the mystery must be provided. The trick is to slowly reveal everything, yet still surprise the reader.
2. *The crime must be significant.* The stealing of a fishing pole could be significant to a twelve-year-old character and reader, but an adult will need something stronger, something that will make him care that the crime is solved and the criminal brought to justice.
3. *There must be several suspects known to the reader, and the guilty party must be among this number.* Sometimes the suspects are obvious, as in a locked room mystery. Sometimes they are not as clearly delineated, but the reader must be satisfied that the criminal, when unmasked, was a viable candidate from his first introduction.
4. *There must be detection.* Clues both true and false must be strewn about. Logical progression of thought must be seen.

   Motives must abound. Several characters must have the opportunity to commit the crime. Unanswered questions must stalk both the detective and the reader before the resolution satisfies both.
5. *All surprises in the story must spring from the universe of the story.* The writer cannot suddenly produce a character, a fact, or a situation unless it grows naturally out of the world the writer has created. Secrets abound in mysteries, and they are part of the fun, but when revealed, the reader must nod her head and say, "I should have seen it coming!"

In a mystery, as in all fiction, good news is bad news for your story, and bad news is good. Novelist John Irving says, "Develop the best possible people and have the worst possible things happen to them."

In other words, we must devise conflict on a scale that will hold our readers' attention. Whether our mysteries are character-driven or plot-driven, we must create trouble, trouble, and more trouble.

Some of the trouble will be intrinsic to the character, an inner turmoil that would exist even without the mystery. The rest of the plot comes from the external arena of crime, detection, and struggles for life.

It's all these conflicts that create the lifeblood of a good story—*suspense*. What's going to happen? When's it going to happen? Who's it going to happen to? How will it affect the main character? How will it affect me, the reader?

Part of our job as mystery writers is to create as much anxiety and apprehension, as much tension and suspense, as possible. We want to make our readers sweat or bite their nails or stay awake until 3 A.M. because they just had to know whodunit.

Ruth Cavin, mystery editor at St. Martin's Press, said, "What creates suspense is a threat. There must be the prospect of something really bad happening *unless*...." And that's where we writers come in; we create both the threat and the "unless."

The most obvious way to create suspense is *to introduce a problem but leave it unresolved*, at least for some time.

Caroline finds a book, written in code, in the attic of recently deceased Great-Uncle Willy. Its pages are smeared with dark stains. Blood? If so, how did it get all over the book? Is it Great-Uncle Willy's blood? Or someone else's? If so, whose? What does the book say? Why is it in code? What kind of danger is Caroline in because she has found the book? How does she go about solving its mystery?

Unanswered questions. Unresolved problems.

Another way to create suspense is *to use well the viewpoint from which the story is being told*. In a single viewpoint mystery, whether it's first or third person, knowledge is limited to the main character. Caroline finds this book in Willy's attic. When someone breaks into the house while she's at Willy's funeral, she doesn't know whether it's a general robbery like the police say or whether someone is after the codebook. Who was the young man at the funeral home whom she could swear she saw running down the back alley behind Uncle Willy's? When her brakes fail, is it coincidence that it happens while she's receiving threatening phone calls? Why won't the police take her seriously?

It's Caroline's not knowing that creates the tension and the suspense for the reader. For both Caroline and the reader, dangers strike unexpectedly. For both, red herrings and genuine clues appear equally valid, and characters appear equally confusing. Neither she nor the reader knows more or less than the other. Solving the mystery is a joint venture.

In a multiple viewpoint version of the same mystery, the reader is with Uncle Willy as he hides the codebook. The reader is with Caroline as she finds it after Willy's death. The reader is with Hans Werner as he searches Willy's house during the funeral and almost gets caught by a young thief dressed in black. The reader is with the young thief as he goes straight to the attic, only to find the codebook gone. The reader is with Caroline when she comes home from the funeral sooner than expected. The reader is with Sgt. Jurgen of the local police as he tells Caroline it's a routine funeral robbery even though he knows it's not.

The reader follows the thought processes and actions of many characters, aware of the plans hatched by each against the other, always wondering how Caroline can escape the mayhem, and how things can ever resolve successfully. The interplay of all these people, each knowing something slightly different and doing something slightly different, and the uncertainty about how all these actions and issues will merge successfully at the resolution, creates the tension and suspense.

Phyllis Whitney, prolific writer of romantic suspense novels, suggests that giving your characters secrets that they will go to great lengths to protect can heighten suspense. Here are some examples:

> Caroline knew Uncle Willy as a kind and thoughtful man who had been especially nice to her after her parents' deaths, even paying for her last two years of college and bankrolling her until she became established as a journalist.
>
> *Secret:* Uncle Willy was a Gestapo officer during World War II. He used papers stolen from a man he had killed to come to America as a displaced person. The codebook in the attic indicates the hiding place of stolen art treasures.

> Caroline knew Hans Werner as a friend of Uncle Willy's, not one of her favorite people, but certainly not anyone to fear.
>
> *Secret:* Hans Werner was a ruthless junior officer under Uncle Willy's command when the treasures were stolen from a French museum and hidden. He oversaw the deaths of the curator and his assistant without a second thought.

Caroline knew Sgt. Jurgen as the man who responded when she called in the robbery report, the brake failure, and the threatening phone calls. He was efficient, professional, and disinterested.

Secret: Sgt. Jurgen was the son of a German Jew, Guenther Jurgen, who had escaped Europe fifty years ago. Uncle Willy had allowed Guenther and his ill Gentile wife to escape when Guenther bought their freedom by turning in a Jewish family and the Gentiles who were hiding them.

Caroline knew the thief in black only as a man who came to the funeral, disappeared mid-service, and whom she saw running down the alley behind Uncle Willy's when she returned from the funeral.

Secret: The young man was an academic with a specialty in the long-term effects of war trauma on ordinary survivors. He had interviewed Willy, Hans, and Guenther Jurgen, among others, while conducting primary research for a book. He suspected Willy was not what he claimed, and he wanted to prove it for the sake of his career and reputation.

Secrets and the hidden motivations they provide keep the pot roiling and boiling. Remember, one man's secret is the stuff another brags about. Secrets must be linked to the personalities of the characters.

Every Mystery Contains Three Things: Motive, Means, and Opportunity

Motive is why the crime in your story was committed. Each major character should have some motive to do away with the deceased. One motive, maybe two, per character will do nicely. It is the plenitude of motives that keeps the resolution on hold until the end of the story. Most motives grow out of four basic human emotions: greed, love, pain, and the longing for power. A normal desire—be it for love, money, or authority—becomes warped into a need that the murderer thinks deserves to be met, no matter how, and the end result is murder.

The progression is:

I want it.

I need it.

I deserve it.

I will have it!

Vi knew Uncle Harry had a lot of money and that some day some of it would be hers. For years this knowledge was sufficient. Then social ambition and the desire for power made her begin to eye the money as a present necessity.

"After all the years of waiting around, listening to the old man's boring and repetitious stories, I deserve my money, and I deserve it now!"

As debt mounted because Vi insisted on living like the money was already hers, she began to feel pushed and panicky. It was only a short walk from I-need-and-deserve-this-money to I-will-have-it-now!

In addition to motive, the suspect must have the *means* to commit the crime. It's one thing to yearn for Uncle Harry's demise. It's another thing for Vi to have some way to bump him off. The author must be certain that not only does Vi have access to a weapon and can use it, but she also has some way to dispose of it after the crime. So Vi doesn't stand out as the villain from page one, several other characters must also have means to murder. Perhaps several family members knew Uncle Harry had digitalis in his medicine chest. Perhaps any and all the guests at the house for his eightieth birthday party could have "borrowed" a gun from his collection. Perhaps several could have sneaked in and held a pillow over his face.

Finally, *opportunity* is what allows someone the actual time and place to commit the crime. It does Vi no good to know about the digitalis but never be able to get to it. It does Vi no good to know about the gun collection but never be alone in the room with it and a key. It does her no good to be able to hold a pillow over Uncle Harry's face if his private duty nurses never leave him alone so she can do it.

Opportunity is what the police try to establish when they check on alibis. Obviously, if Vi is somewhere else when the old man dies, then she hasn't the opportunity to kill him even though she has a motive (the money) and the means (the digitalis, the gun, or the pillow).

Motive indicates you've a reason to commit the crime.

Means indicates you've a method available to do it.

Opportunity means you could have done it because you were at the critical place at the critical time.

Clues May Be Presented in Several Different Ways

Clues should be little tidbits of data the writer provides for the reader to help him solve the mystery. These hints and facts, properly interpreted, point to the criminal. However, much of the information provided is spurious, designed to confuse the issue and complicate the story. We call these false clues "red herrings." The term comes from the smoked herring that was dragged across a trail to try and confuse hounds being trained for fox hunting. To the writer, the real clues and the red herrings seem so obvious, but when they're surrounded by murder, suspense, romance, chases, fear, attempted murder, blackmail, and other mystery staples, they are not obvious at all.

Misdirection

Misdirection is the method of confusing the issue. As soon as a real clue is casually dropped, something else happens to draw the reader's attention.

A man is dead. Suddenly his frowsy wife perks up and becomes a very stylish widow.

> "Jodie," Mac said, frowning. "What's different about you?" Jodie smiled shyly. "Makeup. Darren didn't like me to wear it." Mac reached to push the partially closed den door open. "Well, you look love..." He halted abruptly, and Jodie walked into him. "What's wrong?" She tried to see around him. He shifted position, hoping to block her line of sight. "Let's go into the kitchen and get a cup of coffee." But her indrawn breath and her quick about face told him that she'd seen her twenty-year-old daughter deep in the embrace of Ken Wiley, an embrace that held nothing of the consoler and much of the lover. She spun back to Mac and hissed, "He's old enough to be her father!"

There follows a scene of accusations, recriminations, and tears. One of these clues is very important; the rest are misdirection. The valuable clue is the makeup Jodie is now wearing. The average reader won't be able to discern what is important and what things are red herrings, hopefully, until the end of the book.

Hidden Clues

Clues may be hidden in clusters of things. A drawer's contents, the collection of things in a woman's purse, or a man's pockets contain one vital thing among the others. The beauty of clusters is that the reader can't possibly discern what is important and what isn't, even if he could remember all the items after he turns the page, which he can't.

To make the suspense of this type of clue last as long as possible, the individual items in the cluster must all be things that could logically be found in this place.

> Gordon dumped the purse on the kitchen table. Was it too much to hope that the contents would tell him something significant about this woman?
>
> A lipstick; a compact; a train schedule; an empty address book; a button; a letter stamped but unaddressed; three pens advertising Dr. Henry Blauden, Chiropractor; a paperback mystery with a library due card in it; and no wallet. He stared at the sorry clump of items, looking for something, anything that would make sense of her senseless killing.

A good mystery writer will have the hero/heroine examine all the clues in the cluster, some of which will immediately be dead ends, some of which should have possibilities. Any reader who has seen Cary Grant and Audrey Hepburn in *Charade* thinks the clue is the stamp. However if I were writing this book, the clue would be the library due card. The book was not signed out by the victim, as the microfilm taken at the library will prove, but by the murderer who left the book when he fled. Just such a clue enabled the police to capture a true-life murderer in our area not long ago.

Hidden-in-Plain-Sight Clues

Clues may be hidden in plain view. Edgar Allen Poe used this device in "The Purloined Letter" when the letter being searched for was sitting openly on the desk with the rest of the mail.

The same gimmick could work with missing keys hanging on the key rack in the kitchen or a rare book in the stack of titles waiting to be returned to the library. Because keys belong on the key rack and books belong in a pile to be returned, no one looks twice, including the reader.

> Allie paced the room, trying to remember, trying to pull up a replay of the accident.
>
> They said she was there, kneeling beside Grandmother's fallen, broken body. They said she kept saying, "I didn't mean it!" They said she became hysterical when they tried to lead her to her room by way of the grand staircase down which Grandmother had fallen. They said all kinds of things.
>
> Allie's hands began to shake, and she grabbed the knitting bag on the floor by Grandmother's chair. Knitting always calmed her, just as it had calmed Grandmother. Knit a row, purl a row. No thought required.
>
> She untangled a knot in the yarn and began the rhythmic knit-purl movement. After a while, some of her tension lessened.

The yarn is the hidden-in-plain-sight murder weapon, tied across the steps for Grandmother to trip over. Sometime Allie will realize the significance of the knot, but not for a long time yet.

Character Clues

Clues grow out of character. While our murderer may be hiding behind a curtain of charm and humor, clues must be subtly planted that reveal the manipulating, demanding nature beneath the charm.

> "And where are you going, Charlotte, my love?"
>
> She froze at the sound of his voice. Why wasn't he at the office?
>
> "Out," she said, hoping her voice sounded firm and assured.
>
> He smiled. She hated his smile.
>
> "Not today, my dear." He was the very picture of consideration. "You know you haven't been feeling well, and I'm afraid you are heading for Haven's Rest again. You need your rest and your medicine."
>
> He took her arm and turned her. "Up the stairs now. Into bed. We don't want you falling apart in public, do we?"

Poor Charlotte. She may well end up dead because her husband fears that he is losing control of her. She was actually trying to leave the house on her own. Perhaps she will try to leave him next. He cannot allow that because he needs her money and he fears what she can tell people about him. Under his smarmy charm and false concern beats a larcenous coward's heart.

Or, he could turn up dead because she has become desperate to escape him and can think of no other way to guarantee her freedom from his suffocation and manipulation.

Either way, character is a clue.

Clues may also be found in something overheard, something found, something that doesn't belong, someone's unusual behavior, or a certain location. The trick is to keep adding clue after clue so that your reader is kept off balance and uncertain.

We know we have written a successful mystery if at the conclusion of the book our reader says with great satisfaction, "Of course! I should have known. It was all there all the time."

Communicating Spiritual Truths Through Christian Fiction

10

by Carole Gift Page

If words are to enter men's minds and bear fruit, they must be the right words shaped cunningly to pass men's defenses and explode silently and effectually within their minds.

—J. B. Phillips

During its infancy some twenty or thirty years ago, Christian fiction had a reputation (deserved or undeserved) of being primarily a vehicle for delivering a message or preaching a sermon. (And often the vehicle seemed a rattletrap rather than a Cadillac!)

Like the old-time Tom Mix westerns, you could tell the good guys in their white hats from the bad guys in their black Stetsons. In much Christian fiction, the good guys were the "saved" and the bad guys the "unsaved," until the saved saved the unsaved, and they joined the ranks of the saved.

I say this tongue-in-cheek not to impugn Christian fiction, but rather to point out a typical operating principle of that time when

Christians could do no wrong and non-Christians could do no right. Such stories often tidily concluded with the non-Christians accepting the Lord and living "happily ever after."

The problem with such stories was that everyone, especially non-Christian readers, recognized that life simply didn't work that way. While Christ saves us instantly for eternity, He gives us a lifetime to learn how to live in the power of His Holy Spirit. Sometimes the lessons are hard, painful, and must be learned over and over again. To loosely paraphrase the Apostle Paul: What we know we should do, we don't do; and what we know we shouldn't, we do!

In the last decade, Christian fiction has matured, growing more sophisticated, appealing to a broader audience, and expanding into new genres. Christian bookstores now boast shelves of Christian romances, mysteries, westerns, fantasy, science fiction, and historical novels. Indeed, in the Christian publishing industry, fiction has gone from being a poor cousin to a favorite son. Twenty years ago only the bravest published novels; today most have a fiction line. Why? Because they sell.

Amid such success, we as Christian fiction writers must be careful not to forget our original purpose in writing Christian fiction. You may express it differently, but I believe our goal is to reveal the person of Christ and show what He can do in a heart surrendered to Him amid a chaotic world. However we may define them, how are we communicating spiritual truths?

Most of us have come a long way from portraying our characters as all good or all bad, or as melodramatic caricatures such as Miss Goody Two-Shoes versus the Evil Professor/Mad Scientist. Some of us, in an effort to write for the "crossover" (secular) market, have eliminated all religious jargon. However, in the process of whitewashing our manuscripts for a secular readership, we may have erased the spiritual themes and issues that originally drew us to Christian fiction.

How do we maintain that necessary balance of conveying life-changing truths without sounding preachy?

In this chapter, let us explore effective ways of communicating spiritual truths in fiction, starting with these dos and don'ts:

Don't Try to Be Pious Just for the Sake of Piety

You'll turn off your readers every time, even the religious ones, if you try to act pious. When I started writing stories for the Sunday school take-home papers over twenty years ago, I thought it was my duty to be pious, so I crammed every spiritual truth I could into every story. Fortunately, during our weekly critique sessions, my fellow writer-friend, Doris Elaine Fell—a no-nonsense former missionary—promptly eliminated any hint of overblown piety from my work. I'm convinced what remained came across as immensely more natural, honest, and palatable to the reader.

Don't Let Spirituality Come Too Easily for Your Characters

If we're honest, most of us will admit our spiritual lives leave much to be desired. Often, the more sensitive and attuned we become to the voice of God, the more we realize how much we have to learn and how far we have to travel in our spiritual journey. The more honestly we can paint the subtle shades and nuances of our walk with Christ, the more we will strike a responsive chord in our readers.

Have you noticed? When you hear the testimonies of so-called "spiritual giants," you're often inspired more by the struggles they've faced than the victories they've achieved. Spirituality that is attained too easily seems suspect. So it is with your fictional characters. If you arbitrarily "save" them without showing the awareness and motivation that led to their decision, your reader may feel cheated. After all, it's easy enough for a writer to simply say something is so; it's another matter to demonstrate how your character's spiritual hunger grows to the point of his accepting Christ as his Savior.

The principle is the same in showing your character's spiritual growth after his conversion. Don't just claim he's a Peter or a Paul; show the hard road of faith and discipline he walked to get there. Don't show her living above temptations; show her being tempted but resisting, with God's help. Or if she yields to temptation, show her struggling to make things right again with God and growing through the process.

In the following passage from *Summer of a Stranger*, my second teen novel in "The Kasey Carlone Series" (Moody Press), Kasey's "missionary dating" backfires when the boy makes a pass at her:

> She looked up at him. "People can let you down, but not God. He loves you, Dusty, and He wants the best for you."

"I wish I could believe that, but so far I haven't seen much evidence of God's love in my life."

"Maybe you just haven't been looking for it. Maybe His love has been there waiting for you all the time."

Dusty bent over and kissed her forehead. "If anybody could make me believe that, Kasey, it'd be you." Carefully he removed her glasses and ran his finger over her nose and chin. "You make me feel loved, Kasey. I haven't felt that way for a *long, long* time."

She could smell the cherry pie on his breath as he brought his face close to hers. She knew she should get up and run into the house, but she couldn't make herself move.

Then it was too late. His lips were on hers, and he was crushing her against him.

Kasey eventually resists, but her brush with sexual temptation brings spiritual dilemmas she must deal with in the next chapter. She struggles with guilt, questions her own motives, wonders if she'll be able to resist further involvement, and agonizes that her behavior has put a rift between her and the Lord. Only after she prays it out—examining her behavior, confessing her wrongdoing, claiming Christ's forgiveness, and reestablishing her closeness with God—does Kasey recognize the great thing about being a Christian: *Even when she did something wrong, Jesus was ready to forgive her and help her make things right.*

If I'd written this story with a "spiritual" agenda, I might have shown Kasey easily resisting temptation because she's a Christian. But I wanted to keep it honest, true to human nature. Teenage girls know how hard it is to stay pure. In depicting the complexities and contradictions of Kasey's sexual and spiritual struggles, I tried to communicate, with a balance of hope and realism, these important truths:

- Missionary dating usually backfires.
- Be careful. Even when you're sure you can resist, you can't.
- Your behavior is tied to your spiritual life. What you do will affect how close you feel to God.
- Christ is ready to restore that intimate connection with Him when you agree with Him you were wrong and return to the sheltering umbrella of His love.

- As you maintain a close walk with Christ, He can give you strength to obey Him in all areas of your life.

Remember the Complexity of Real Life

Motives, motivations, and behaviors are not always clear-cut or one-sided; rarely are they entirely good or entirely bad. In the novel cited above, Kasey has both good and bad motivations in cultivating her friendship with Dusty. She genuinely wants to see him come to know the Lord. Her innate nurturing spirit wants to comfort him in the loss of his younger brother. She realizes Dusty is a loner. Life has dealt him some nasty blows, and he doesn't find it easy to trust people. She wants to earn his trust and help him deal with some of the deep issues in his life. All of these motives are admirable. However, Kasey is also flattered and dazzled by his attention. He's a handsome, older boy, and she's drawn to him physically. Even when she knows she's getting in over her head, she tells herself she can handle it.

Show Your Characters Learning from and Growing Through Their Spiritual Struggles

In the story above, Kasey becomes a stronger person and a deeper Christian after the incident with Dusty. She is better prepared to handle future sexual temptations, and she has learned that God is faithful to forgive her and restore their close relationship. In fact, communion with Christ is sweeter than before. She has seen God in action as He revealed her wrongdoing, lovingly urged her repentance, freely forgave, and showered her with His love.

Review, Reflect on, and Then Write from Your Own Spiritual Struggles and Victories

Your writing will be more authentic when you write from your own needs and personal discoveries. In my novel, *Family Reunion* (Crossway Books), about a minister returning home for the deathwatch of his father, I had an opportunity to explore personal spiritual issues. My main character, Justin, faces a crisis of faith after his father's death. In the following scene, as he prays alone in his boyhood home, Justin confronts himself more honestly than ever before and comes through with a deeper understanding of his walk with God:

Where was the Holy Spirit when he needed Him? Where was the source of inner power and strength? He knew the textbook answers, but they weren't enough for him now when everything in his life seemed so out of focus.

Or perhaps he was being too analytical, too introspective. It was a habit of his, analyzing everything to death, seeking the hidden meaning of things when perhaps there was none.... He realized he had the peculiar habit of viewing his life from two perspectives—first person, through his own eyes; and third person, through the eyes of a detached and mildly skeptical bystander....

At this moment he wasn't *Rev. Justin Cahill, man of God*. He was simply *Justin, a man in need*, who painfully felt the limitations and shortcomings of his humanity.

Was this what he had come to after so many years of trying to be Christ-like?... "It can only happen when...I open myself to Him with nothing held back.... Lord, do I want to be more like You than like myself? More like You than like my father? ...How much of what I see in You is really myself? How much of what I know of You is only me? Where do I leave off and You begin? And how can I know the difference? How can I truly serve you when I glimpse You only through...my own flawed understanding?"

...There were so few times that anything he did was out of a pure motive; weren't his motives always a mixture of good and evil—wanting to help someone but also wanting to boost his self-esteem, wanting his sermons to draw people to Christ while he also desired admiration for himself? Did his flawed motives negate the good he tried to accomplish?

Only as Justin recalls his childhood faith does he break through the emotional barriers that bind him:

It had been many years since Justin's faith had been childlike, many years since he had felt like a child at the feet of Jesus. But, surprisingly, he felt that way now. And why not? He had just been orphaned. He was a fatherless child. He had only his Heavenly Father to cling to now.

> He became aware of a feeling inside that he had felt only rarely in his life-a deep, gnawing hunger for Christ's presence. He ached for the Spirit to cleanse and fill him.... He felt a sob rising in his chest. It convulsed inside him, but there were no tears, only a dry, heaving anguish. He was in the throes of struggling with God and he must see it through to the finish.

Justin is confronted with the same question Jesus asked Peter: "Do you love Me?" Like Peter, he dodges its deeper implications until he meets Christ at the heart level as well as the intellectual:

> Tears came at last, freely, unchallenged, unguarded. "Oh, God, I don't know. Have I loved You? Or have I loved only myself? How long since I've really seen You...focused only on You...felt love for You flaming in my heart?"

At last Justin seeks God's forgiveness, saying:

> "Forgive me for trying to be You instead of simply loving You and letting You be Yourself through me.... I love You, Jesus."
>
> He felt the spaces of his heart swelling with Christ's Spirit, filling to overflowing. He felt one with God, one in purpose, one in sweet communion.... It was too good, too satisfying to let it slip away. All of life's turmoil, struggles, and perplexities were worth the bliss of having all his senses attuned to Christ.

The passage above showing Justin's renewed emotional connection with his Savior leads naturally to our next point.

Capture the Passion of Our Love Relationship with Christ

Don't be guilty of boring your readers with the most exciting news on earth—the Good News of Christ. Don't focus only on the intellectual, clinical, or pedantic in writing about spiritual truths. Communicate the excitement of a growing, changing, thriving, glorious, intimate relationship with the Lover of our souls.

Virginia Muir, former editor of Tyndale House, warns, "All too many writers are devoid of passion: that urgency of concern and overflow of eagerness, of fervor, ardor, warmth, zeal...of *fire*. Unless our own blood is stirring, our own hearts beating fast, surely no reader will experience a surge of response."

Show, Don't Preach

We have an advantage in Christian fiction that nonfiction writers don't have. We already know we're supposed to "Show, Don't Tell." Nonfiction writers may tell people what to do, what to believe, and how to live. But fiction offers a different platform. We don't (or shouldn't) preach, scold, admonish, or lecture. Rather, we bring characters on stage and let them demonstrate through their actions what life is and what works and doesn't work. Readers learn by example.

Share the Experience

Don't write from a contrived, predetermined agenda; write with an open, tender heart, sharing experience and seeking truth.

Let me reiterate. Our objective is not to tell another person what to do or how to think. Let experience speak. Your experience. Your characters' experiences. Remember, your story may be contrived, but the truths, feelings, and experiences you bring to your reader must be genuine. As a fiction writer, you are free to arrange the "facts," but the feelings must ring true to the core of your own emotions. In dealing with experience and human responses, you must be scrupulously honest. Write from your own vulnerabilities, your own hard-won victories and bitter failings. Write from your rawest, heartfelt need. Be honest to the point of pain. But above all: *Share the experience*.

Famed fiction writer W. Somerset Maugham declared, "To be told what some man thinks life should mean to us may interest but is not likely to move us deeply or to change us. But to be *shown*, vitally and vividly, what life has meant to any human being can hardly fail to reach our emotions and to affect the whole mental being. Life can teach more than any man can teach."

Strive to Make Virtue as Exciting as Vice

In an article titled, "It's Universally Easy to Describe Vice and Hard to Depict Virtue," columnist Sydney Harris points out, "In every language, there are dozens and dozens of synonyms for such words as *lying, stealing, and drunkenness*, but very few words for their virtuous opposites."

Harris continues, "In Milton's great epic, 'Paradise Lost,' you cannot but be impressed with the fact that Satan is the most vividly drawn and compelling character in that long poem. Even though Milton loved God and hated Satan, as a literary artist he found it impossible to translate his feelings accurately. Satan remains the most fascinating figure Milton ever drew."

Harris also claims the great novelist Dostoyevsky "fails to give his saints the impact his sinners have." The same can be said for Shakespeare's rogues and villains.

In attempting to explain why bad characters are often so much more vivid than good ones, Harris quotes William Hubben in his book, *Four Prophets of Our Destiny*:

> "It is so easy to define evil and portray the sinner with concrete accuracy, because evil and sin are finite and human.
>
> "But virtue, perfection, and saintliness elude us because they reach out into the infinite realm of eternity. We can only touch them slightly or sense the direction of their moving energies....
>
> "Writers are 'at their best' when they portray the worst, just as critics are most readable when they are destructive—just as we can describe something we hate with passionate fluency, but become tongue-tied in trying to express our love or admiration. And every language in every land reflects the same failure to articulate the infinite."

We may escape some of this dilemma if we're careful not to categorize our characters solely as saints or sinners, but rather as human beings in various stages of seeking and surrendering themselves to God or wrestling against Him. Still, we as Christian writers may have no greater challenge than this—to render our vast, illimitable God in such a way that He can be glimpsed and embraced by the needy human heart.

Accept the Challenge to Reflect His Infinity

Jessica Shaver penned one of the finest challenges I've read for Christian authors. Directed at poets, it's equally applicable for writers of Christian fiction. In an article titled, "Pass the Literary Whipped Cream," Jessica speaks of Christian poetry being disappointing:

"...a flat excuse for a moral. Instead of forces within the poet sandpapering granular struggles and longings into pearls, Christian poetry seemed neatly and synthetically created around standard grains of sand.

"Where are the Christian artists, poets, and novelists who are saying and asking great things—and doing it honestly, not always with answers? ...Where is contemporary Christian literature?...

"Through literature, I connect with kindred spirits who sampled life before me and found it good, tragic and difficult, who not only marveled at dewdrops on spider webs but lashed out at the God they loved for seeming silent in their grief....

"Where are the beauty-makers who call us to rise up and follow, to reach toward excellence creatively because we are made in the image of a Creator-God? Where are His people who have the courage to fill voids that have been tiptoed around?

"Where are you, reflector of His infinity, who trembles with desire to produce something original for Him?

"Do we dare risk breaking out of the conventional, risk stretching beyond what feels safe?

"In T. S. Eliot's 'The Love Song of J. Alfred Prufrock,' the agonizingly timid Prufrock asks,'Do I dare disturb the universe?'

"Do we?"

I echo her sentiment. In the first century, Jesus' disciples turned the world upside down with their zeal to spread the Gospel. What can we-thousands of Christian writers across this country—accomplish for Christ in our post-Christian world during our lifetimes?

Eight Ways to Add More Hours to Your Writing Day

11

by Donna Clark Goodrich

Self-employed persons have to work only half a day. It's up to them to decide which twelve hours it will be.

—Author Unknown

As a writer, you are self-employed. However, many writers—Christian writers especially—are also employed full-time. They struggle to fit writing time around their eight-to-five job, along with juggling home and family responsibilities.

If you're one who has cried, "I don't have time to write," this chapter is for you. It may be that you don't need *more* time; rather, that you be a better steward of the time you have. How can you do this?

Prioritize Your Tasks

Our pastor told us that if we followed one rule, we could change our lives in a week. "Every night before you go to bed, make a list of what you have to do the next day," he said. "Then rearrange the list in order of priority."

I tried it. I wrote out my list and put the jobs in order of priority, but it didn't work. Why? Because I didn't *do* them in my written order of priority. I skipped through the list picking out those *I wanted to do.*

Then I read about a writer who made a similar list, but she made it a practice to complete the top three jobs on that list every day. I tried that, too. My problem, however, was that the first time I made out my list and rearranged the items in order, I had thirty-nine jobs jumping out at me. I did what I could the first day, and then recopied the list for the second day, adding a few new jobs. I felt all I was doing every day was recopying the same list, with a few changes and/or additions.

I've finally found a method that works for me; perhaps it will help you, too. I now make my list at the beginning of the week, then, depending on my schedule for the week, I assign jobs to specific days. If I'm working on a big project, I break it into smaller pieces for that day's schedule. This makes it more manageable to complete my list each day.

In her book *15 Minutes Alone with God* (Harvest House Publishers), Emily Barnes suggests, "List only those things that need to be done today, not tomorrow or next week, but just today."

Plan Your Schedule

Writers who do not work outside of the home often say it is as difficult for them to find time to write as someone with a forty-hour-a-week job, because of the interruptions. The secret is to plan your writing schedule around those interruptions, or use the interruptions to your advantage.

For example, I schedule my jobs depending on whether I'm going to be home, what's happening at home that week, or if I have to run errands. Jobs that require use of the computer are scheduled for days I'm home. Editing jobs are for early mornings and late evenings when it's quiet because I have a disabled husband at home. If I require more time I use my "away" office—a back table in a hospital cafeteria where my daughter works. Fast-food restaurants and the library also work great as "away" offices.

Jobs that don't require as much concentration, such as research, scanning sample magazines, addressing and stuffing envelopes, or writing rough drafts in pencil, I do while I watch a favorite program on TV. Time spent with my husband in doctors' waiting rooms is used to write, read magazines or books, or edit manuscripts.

If you work away from home, write during your breaks or lunch hour. If you carpool or ride the bus or subway, use the time to write or edit manuscripts. If you pick up your children at school or your mate at work, go fifteen minutes early and work while you wait.

Use the time you spend waiting in line at the supermarket to study the magazines on the racks. Read the titles; see what type of articles various magazines use on a regular basis. Watch and listen to the people talking around you. This is a good idea in a doctor's office or in other public locations, too. Fifteen minutes a day, five days a week adds up to sixty-five hours a year—and that's a lot of extra time to write.

Set Goals

One author, who finds it difficult to carve out a block of time in a day, prefers to set a goal of writing two articles a week or a certain number of pages. This gives her the freedom to choose which hours or days she will write. Other writers set aside one day a week or a specific period, perhaps a week at a time.

What works for you? Regardless of what you hear at every writers' seminar, there is nothing magic about "one or two hours a day." Don't put yourself on a guilt trip if you have younger children, a sick spouse, or aging parents who take up your time. Sometimes you'll find you can't spare as much time every day as you would like. Can you find one afternoon or evening a week? Can you exchange childcare with another writer? Can a neighbor or friend sit with your spouse or parent for a few hours while you go to the library?

Members of a local writers club set goals for themselves to be met before the next meeting. These may include: reading a book on writing, updating marketing files, outlining an article, sending out a query letter, or completing a chapter of a book—anything connected with writing.

Do you want to write a book? Itemize what needs to be done *before* you start writing. What research do you need to do? Who will you need to interview? Now set a goal for each month. For example: By the end of January you'll complete the research for Chapter 1. Even with limited time, you can finish this book. One page a day will give you a 365-page first draft of a book at the end of the year. Or strive for five pages on a weekend. Long-range goals could include sending out ten articles or stories a month, taking a correspondence course in writing, or setting up a marketing file.

If you have a number of projects in mind and don't know where to begin, make a list and study it. Which project is the most important to you? Which matters most to God? Which book, article, story, or poem does a hurting world need today? Decide and start writing.

Organize

You don't have to own the cleanest office in town, but you do need to know where things are.

A file cabinet is a simple method of organization. Buy one at a "crash and dent" sale; it doesn't matter what it looks like. Set up files for clippings, for ideas, for manuscripts, for sample magazines, for workshop notes, and an "A to Z" file for correspondence.

Clippings

Make it a habit to read newspapers and magazines with a clipper and pen. When you cut out an article, immediately write the source, the date, and the topic on the top to be filed at your convenience.

Ideas

As soon as you get an idea for a story or article, give it a working title and set up a folder. Later, when other ideas come to you or you find related quotations, add them to the file. Throwing it into a box of "Ideas" will only slow you down on the day when you find a few precious moments to write.

Magazines and Guidelines

These can be filed alphabetically in a file drawer or cardboard box. Or you can file them by category: women's magazines, children's, family, and so on.

Manuscripts

Always know the status of your manuscripts. I keep two logs: a manuscript record that I store in the manuscript file and a chronological record that I three-hole punch and put in a notebook. I can look in my manuscript file any time and see where and when any particular article or story was sent out. Or, by checking my notebook, I can see at a glance what is in the mail.

Learn to Say No

A writer in a woman's magazine asked the question, "What are you now doing that someone else can do so you can do what God has called you to do?"

There is nothing wrong with church, school, and community involvements, but what takes precedence in your life? Do these jobs crowd out what God wants you to do?

Jan Johnson wrote that she reached the point where her "good" concerns crowded out her "best" ones. So many things appealed to her, that she kept committing herself to projects that left her feeling empty. "I grew afraid," she said, "that I would wake up at the end of my life and wonder why I hadn't accomplished my dreams—or even attempted them."

Don't be afraid to say no. Don't feel guilty when you say no. And don't feel you have to defend yourself. For years, whenever someone asked me to do something, I responded with a long list of my "to do's." It was as though I felt I had to justify my reason for saying no and was too embarrassed to tell that person I wanted to write. One evening I turned down a rush typing job, telling the caller I already had "plans."

"I didn't know you were going somewhere tonight," my husband commented when I hung up. "I'm not," I replied. "My plans are to write." And I felt no guilt!

Forget Writing Occasionally

Sometimes you need to get away from writing entirely and recharge your batteries. In a "Winnie the Pooh" vignette, Rabbit carried a ladder past Pooh and said, "No time for talk, Pooh! I'm busy, busy, busy fixing my roof."

Pooh replied, "My goodness, Rabbit! Don't you ever take time out just to smell the flowers?"

"By George! You're right, Pooh!" Rabbit agreed.

Later, when Piglet stopped to talk, Rabbit breathlessly said, "No time for talk, Rabbit. I'm busy, busy, busy smelling the flowers."

Get away from the computer for awhile. Read a good book. Attend a concert. Watch a favorite TV program. Go for a walk. Take your children or grandchildren to the park or the zoo. Browse the mall. Take time for yourself, and your writing will be better for it!

Treat Your Writing as a Calling from God

Harold Ivan Smith gave a talk at a writers' seminar that literally changed my writing career. Up to that time I had treated writing only as a hobby, to be done when and if I had the time. Then I heard Harold say these words: "We are called to write, and I feel we will be held responsible at the Judgment for the people who are hurting that we could have helped but didn't, because we didn't write what God laid on our hearts to write." That took writing out of the hobby category for me and made it a calling.

I have never heard a preacher say, "I don't have time to prepare my sermon." He takes the time, because God has called him to preach.

In a *Writer's Digest* article titled "How to Finish What You Start—Every Time," Marshall J. Cook said, "If writing is an important part of your life...you need to give it prime time." If a secular writer feels this way, how much more should we—who carry the greatest message in the world—be willing to give God "prime time" in our lives.

Prioritize Your Life

"Isn't this the same as prioritizing your tasks discussed in the first point?" you ask. No, there we talked about prioritizing *tasks*. Now you must determine where writing fits into your life and realize that, at times, some things may come ahead of your writing. These things include:

Friends

A writer friend has a little sign above her computer: "Writing can wait; relationships can't." This lady is an excellent writer and has sold many articles. She is also a compassionate person, and people often knock at her door for counseling and prayer.

I'm not saying that you should allow others to constantly interrupt your writing time for trivial reasons. You need to be firm and tell them you are working. However, when a friend or loved one has a need that can't wait, your writing can.

Family

One summer I was unpacking at a writers' seminar when another instructor came into my room. Although we hadn't seen each other in several years, we had kept in touch through a writers' prayer letter.

"How's your family? And how's your writing?" she asked.

I filled her in on my husband's latest health problems. Then, in answer to her second question, I replied, "I'm getting so frustrated in my writing. I just don't have time. I've been so busy taking care of my family."

My friend then said four words that changed my entire outlook. When I said I had been busy caring for my family, she replied, "God will honor that." Normally I would return home after conferences feeling guilty because I wasn't writing as much as I wanted to, but her four words gave me a new perspective.

On another day when I was complaining that I didn't have time to write, a sobering thought came to me: "Someday you'll have all the time you want, and you won't want it!"

One of our family's favorite songs is "We Have This Moment Today." In the chorus, Bill Gaither reminds us that yesterday is gone and that tomorrow may never come. Your children are only young once; your parents are aging rapidly; your spouse needs you. Allow room for them in your writing schedule. I truly believe that if God gives you something to write, He will help you find the time to write it.

In her talk entitled, "Keeping the Sparkle in Your Writing," Sally Stuart warned, "You can't write from an empty cup."

What sets—or should set—you apart from a secular writer is that you have first been touched by God. It's easy to rely solely on your own talent when beginning a project without first asking for God's guidance in what you should write, how you should write it, and where you should send it.

Someone else said it this way: "Go to your knees before you go to your typewriter." Don't leave God out of your writing.

Prioritize your life and put writing in its proper place.

How do you find time to write? The minutes are there waiting. Make the best use of them. If you are called to write, God will help you make time for this important calling.

12 Copyright Law: What You Don't Know Can Cost You

by Cecil Murphey

To have integrity in the media business today means only to be "objective," which has become a code word for having no convictions.

—Susan Faludi

What if Someone Steals My Article?

"But what if someone steals it?" she asked.

By *it*, she was talking about her newly finished article, and she also had an idea for a novel that she referred to as "so original no one has ever thought of it before."

"You can't protect your ideas by copyright," I said and then shocked her by adding, "and you can't even copyright your title, a plot, short phrases, slogans, or the news." I also pointed out that people can't copyright material consisting entirely of information that is common property and contains no original authorship, such as standard calendars, height and weight charts, tape measures and rulers, and lists or tables taken from public documents or other common sources.

"Once your article is in a fixed format," I said, "it's automatically protected by the copyright law."

"What's a fixed format?"

"That's the legal term, but it means when you're finished with the article—when you've stopped editing."

I continued to explain, "The law doesn't require you to do anything to protect your manuscript, whether published or not. Under common law, the copyright is automatically yours, no matter when you started to work on it. And as soon as it is finished, it's automatically copyrighted."

"But what if someone steals my material and publishes it as theirs?"

"They've broken the law." My answer sounded simplistic, but that's probably the best I could offer. This is a question many beginners worry about—probably unnecessarily. As one of my friends put it, "Good writers are too busy writing, and they don't have time to steal." He also added, "The people who worry the most about their material are those who have the most unoriginal things to say and wouldn't tempt anyone." His attitude was a bit caustic, but probably it's close to the truth.

I don't know any instances where others have lifted entire book-length manuscripts and claimed them as their own, because the best literary thieves usually steal only portions. Occasionally, they'll take an article, but if they're clever, they'll disguise the material enough that there's little chance of being detected. If they change enough words and use different illustrations, the most that anyone can say is that they stole the idea. And, again, no one can copyright ideas.

In one famous case, romance writer Janet Dailey lifted entire pages of dialogue from Nora Roberts, changing only a few words. She got caught when one devotee of both authors noticed the repeated material in Dailey's books. So far as I know, that's the exception.

Another worry I hear occasionally is, "If I send my article to a magazine and they like the idea, they may reject my piece and choose one of their favorite writers to write it. Then all I get is a rejection slip."

That's possible, and some editors may do that, but I believe they're a minority. Ethical editors wouldn't intentionally behave that way. "Think about it like this," I said. "An editor may read your articles in

August—yours and three hundred others—and sends you a rejection. The following April, that same editor might think of an article for her magazine that's similar to the idea you proposed. At this point, she doesn't remember your article, and she assigns the project to another writer. Or she may have assigned such a topic to a writer *before* receiving your manuscript. Such things happen."

I also pointed out that sometimes we get an idea and assume we're the only person in the entire universe who has such a clever idea. Almost any editor will tell you that ideas seem to go in phases.

If you're seriously worried about theft of your material or ideas, this chapter probably won't help. Here are two reasons:

1. Publishers committed to theft will steal your idea but disguise it enough that no court can convict them.
2. Ideas are everywhere. A friend once said, "Every day, God stands above the universe and throws down five new ideas. Those who are attuned, grab the ideas first." It's quite possible that others do have similar ideas for an article or a book.

So far as I know, no one has ever stolen any of my work, and I've been publishing for more than twenty-five years. I've heard a few horror stories, but they involved screenplays and Hollywood.

The reality is that there's probably no way to protect yourself from the unscrupulous. Thieves will always find opportunities to steal.

Even so, all writers still need to know the basics of copyright law. Here are the essentials for writers to understand about copyright. Consult a lawyer who specializes in copyright law if you have additional questions.

What Is Copyright Law?

Copyright is a form of protection provided by the laws of the United States (Title 17, U.S. Code) to the authors of "original works of authorship" including literary, dramatic, musical, artistic, and other intellectual works. This protection is available to both published and unpublished works. From Section 106 of the Copyright Act, here are three important exclusive rights for published and unpublished works. You have the right to:

- Reproduce your own copyrighted work.
- Prepare derivative works based on the copyrighted work.
- Distribute copies of the copyrighted work to the public by sale, rental, lease, loan, or transfer of ownership.

In short, you have the right to do what you want with your material, such as turn it into another literary form, read from it, or make money from what you've written. When you sell a book manuscript to a publisher, they normally register the copyright as part of the contract. And most magazines are copyrighted, so you are doubly protected when your material appears in an issue.

One area of confusion about copyright involves putting the copyright symbol on manuscripts. Before March 1, 1989, the use of the notice was mandatory on all published works. Any work first published before that date had to bear a notice. Not to do so meant risking the loss of copyright protection. For anything completed or published after March 1, 1989, the use of the copyright notice is optional. Regardless of whether you use the copyright symbol or don't use it, if anyone copies, excerpts, adapts, or publishes your material without permission, they have violated your copyright.

"A common misconception is that you must register a work with the U.S. Copyright Office for it to be protected by copyright. Under present law, copyright exists *automatically* from the moment a work is fixed in a tangible medium.... Therefore, registration...is not necessary." According to Lloyd J. Jassin and Steven C. Schechter as stated in *The Copyright Permission and Libel Handbook:*

> "It may not be worth the money involved to win a copyright case in court. If you feel your rights have been violated, at least contact the 'author' and the publisher. If you decide to go to court, you must prove two facts:
>
> 1. A substantial similarity exists between the two works.
> 2. There is evidence that the infringers took your protected material and used it as their own."

Still worried? Then you can go through statutory copyright process and register your work. Currently the cost is thirty dollars for each piece you register. If your rights are violated, a legal copyright provides additional protection (specifically, the possibility of recovering punitive damages in an infringement suit) as well as legal proof of the date of copyright. Otherwise you are protected by the common law copyright. The intent of the law means simply this: *The work became yours as soon as you created it, and no one else can legally make use of it.*

If you choose to register your material, contact the Copyright Office. They don't give legal advice, but they provide forms and circulars. Call the Office Recorded Information line at 202-707-3000; if you want forms, pamphlets, or circulars, call the Copyright Hotline at 202-707-9100, (fax) 202-707-2600. You can also write to the Copyright Office, Library of Congress, Washington, D.C., 20559-6000 or download forms by connecting to the Library of Congress home page: http://www.loc.gov/ or through the Copyright Office home page: http://www.loc.gov/copyyright.

The present copyright law says that works created after January 1, 1978, are yours for your lifetime plus 70 years. In the case of manuscripts written by two or more authors, the term lasts for 70 years beyond the last surviving author's death. Anything written before 1978 had a copyright of 28 years plus a renewal for another 28, for a total of 56 years. After that, the work went into the public domain.

Fair Use

We can freely quote from material in the public domain—if it really is out of copyright. The law about using works in the public domain refers to *original* works. Here are two examples of how this might confuse writers. First, if someone in 2001 revises or updates a manuscript written in 1801, you can't count the revision as being public domain. Several publishers have updated Christian classics, such as the writings of Oswald Chambers and Charles Spurgeon, and put the new versions under statutory copyright.

Second, Victor Hugo wrote *Les Miserables* in French nearly two hundred years ago. That book is clearly in the public domain. But if you quote from an English translation or a condensation, either may be under copyright. I have a condensed English version produced by CBS, and it is still under copyright.

Before we quote anything for publication, it may be wise to check the copyright date. If you're still unsure about a copyright expiration, contact the Copyright Office.

Quoting from copyrighted material sometimes comes under what we call "Fair Use." The problem is that no one has ever clearly defined what the term means other than to say you can use "a reasonable amount." One lawyer called the idea of fair use the "most troublesome in the copyright world."

So how much is fair? That's where the problem comes in. Some publishers allow 250 words, others 500. Most members of the American University Press Association permit 1,000 so long as you give credit. This rule excludes lyrics, letters, poems, short stories, and essays that are complete units. When in doubt about the amount you can use, query the copyright holder. If you do quote a "reasonable amount," always give credit.

Lawyers argue more over *how* writers use copyrighted material than the amount. You may have quoted only thirty words of an article, but if you quote the heart or core of the article, you may have exceeded fair use. Think of it this way: If you're reviewing or critiquing, you can quote freely from the material. If you're citing a competitive work and want to quote extensively, you need to contact the publisher for permission.

Never use more of a copyrighted work than is necessary to make your point. The more you borrow, the more you face the charge of unfair use. Small amounts, such as my quote above from Lloyd J. Jassin are considered fair usage.

If you wish to quote a story from a published book and the author wants payment, you're the one who pays unless your publisher agrees to do so. Sometimes writer and publisher split the cost. If the owner wants payment, either pay or don't quote the material. You can paraphrase it, but a lawyer friend warned that if the paraphrase is too close to the original, it could be counted as unfair use and a violation of copyright. This is especially true in quoting poems or lyrics.

Here are a few things to remember about fair use:

- You don't need to give credit for a quotation in common use, such as the words of Shakespeare or Lincoln.

- You don't have to get permission to quote short portions from Bible translations.
- You may quote freely from any U.S. government publication without permission, but make sure it's not a reprint of a copyrighted publication. If it is, the copyright remains in force.
- Large libraries have a Catalog of Copyright Entries published by the U.S. Copyright Office. It's usually easy to determine copyright dates from that. Or, for a fee, you can have a record search by contacting the Register of Copyrights, Library of Congress, Washington D.C., 20559.
- For further information, use these two sites: http://lcweb.loc.gov/copyright/title17/; http://arl.cni.org/scomm/copyright/uses.html.

Works for Hire

Section 101 of the copyright statute defines a "work made for hire" as any work done by employees within the scope of their employment. For writers, it means a contract states clearly that the writing is "specially ordered or commissioned" by a publisher. For instance, I have ghostwritten books for several celebrities for which I received a work-for-hire agreement. Once I turned in the material, it was no longer mine, and I had no rights and received no further payments. I list such books on my résumé, but that's the extent of my rights.

Sometimes you can get the copyright back. I did a series of nine devotional books and eleven novels for Fleming H. Revell in the 1980s. Once they went out of print, I wrote and asked for the copyright and the reprint rights to those books. They gave them to me without charge.

Electronic Rights

Now that electronic rights have come on the scene, the laws are still evolving. For instance, on September 24, 1999, the Second Circuit Court of Appeals reversed a federal district court decision, usually cited as the Tasini case. This case involved the *New York Times*, *Newsday*, *Time*, University Microfilms International, and Mead Data Central Corporation (former owner of the Lexis-Nexis electronic databases). The court's unanimous ruling said that publishers *cannot* resell freelancers' work in electronic databases or CD-ROMs without getting permission. The judges ruled that, even when there is no contract relating to electronic rights, a print publisher may not put the writings of freelancers on databases and CD-ROMs that include the entire textual content of the print publication.

This means that freelancers automatically retain electronic rights to their printed works and have sold only their first rights. Writers retain all others, including the right to electronically reproduce their material. For more information, see the following web sites: http://www.nwu.org; www.wemsi.on.ca/netlaw.html and www.bitlaw.com/copyright/.

Definition of Rights

If you have written an article and send it for publication, commonly writers place the rights they sell on the first page, top right-hand corner. Here are the rights you have to sell:

All Rights: This means you sell the material, and you can never resell it unless the publisher returns the rights to you. Your name always remains on the material.

First Rights: Sometimes publishers ask for U.S. North American Rights or first serial rights. Don't let them confuse you. First rights—regardless of the words attached—simply means that the magazine wants to pay to publish your article before anyone else. Once it has appeared in print, it is yours to sell again.

One-time Rights: This means the publisher is asking to publish your article *one* time in *one* publication for *one* fee. This is the same thing as first rights, unless it has been previously published.

Second Rights or Reprint Rights: You sell a magazine the right to publish your article that has been previously published in a periodical. [In books, first serial rights usually refer to excerpts published in a periodical *before* publication of the entire book. Second serial rights refer to excerpts appearing *after* the book's publication.]

Foreign Serial Rights: This refers to articles sold outside North America. Check your contract when you sell an article because it may say these rights belong to the publisher unless you qualify this.

Syndication Rights: This is permission to publish your article, book, or excerpts in more than one newspaper or periodical.

Simultaneous Rights: You sell your material to more than one periodical at the same time. This happens when they are totally noncompeting markets, or it is sold simultaneously to two or more publishers with different circulations.

Subsidiary Rights: This term refers to rights other than those for book publication, such as dramatic rights, book clubs, licensing, and serials. In book publishing, if the publisher sells your hardback book to another publisher for mass marketing, the royalty is usually divided equally between author and publisher.

Rights to New Media: These rights include such things as software and videocassettes.

Work for Hire: You sell all rights, including editorial and copyright. Your name may or may not appear on the published work, depending on the contract.

Rights to Watch For

Reversion Clause: Many books go out of print within a year after publication. If your career should take off five years from now, reprint rights could be invaluable to you.

Some contracts state that after a certain number of years, such as one or five, the rights revert to the author. Ask to have them revert as soon as the publisher declares the book out of print. If they don't agree, urge that the rights must revert within two years.

Subsidiary Rights: Hold onto what are also called "ancillary" or "multi-media" rights. Four of my books, written before I had an agent, sold overseas because a foreign publisher read, liked, and wanted them. One book went out of print in 1985, and a Chinese house picked it up in 1993. Since then, each April I've received a small royalty check.

Retain the rights to audiocassette recordings of your work, a fast-growing area of popularity among a society of commuters. Above all, don't give away the rights to dramatic adaptation, especially movies or TV. Few writers will have their books made into smash Broadway hits or a TV mini-series, but then, who can tell?

Electronic Rights: Still vague and controversial, no one knows where electronic publishing is going, so retain those rights. If the publisher demands them, negotiate a limitation, such as an agreement for a separate advance and royalty. Make sure they're not part of the subsidiary rights split—usually a 50/50 split.

If your publisher wants to create "derivative works in electronic form," resist signing. Today that means CD-ROMs, but in 2005 who knows what will be available? If you give up this right, you lose creative control over the final product.

13 Writing About Yourself

by Lowell S. Saunders

I write with experiences in mind, but I don't write about them, I write out of them.

—John Ashberry

Have you explored the possibilities of writing about yourself? You'd make a great subject!

- You are unique.
- You are valuable.
- You are interesting.
- You are gifted.

From these suppositions follow some logical conclusions. You constitute:

- A worthwhile theme;
- An important theme; and
- An exciting theme for personal writing.

Writing about yourself allows you the roles of both "father" and "mother" in the creative process, because what you write forms an extension of yourself—your "baby"—made in your likeness. Compared to writing for publication, which may bring you a dreaded letter boldly informing you, "We regret that your manuscript does not meet our present needs," writing about yourself can be done without fear of rejection. You can write in your journal, and no one needs to read it. You can craft your autobiography and then seal it for a specific number of years or even forever. In writing, you can explore your various thoughts and deepest longings and let them be known to God alone.

Such personal writing will make your life more significant. You gain insight into the purpose and meaning of your earthly journey. You begin to comprehend more of the grace and mercy of God toward you. What a worthwhile and adequate justification for this form of writing!

Journaling

Did great men and women incidentally keep journals…or in the keeping of journals did they become great?

At one time you may have kept a journal. If you are typical of most people, you feared that someone might discover and read your journal—or diary, as you likely called it—so you hid it under your mattress or behind dusty books on the shelf.

If you do resume or begin keeping a journal, you'll find yourself following a good tradition. King David wrote of the tumultuous events taking place in his life, and many of these became Psalms of sacred Scripture. Here's but one example. Do you recall the time when David's son, Absalom, conspired to take away his father's throne? Absalom went to Hebron and declared himself to be king.

A messenger came and told David, "The hearts of the men of Israel are with Absalom."

> *Then David said to all his officials who were with him in Jerusalem, "Come! We must flee, or none of us will escape from Absalom. We must leave immediately, or he will move quickly to overtake us and bring ruin upon us and put the city to the sword...."*
>
> *The king set out, with his entire household following him....*
>
> *The whole countryside wept aloud as all the people passed by* (2 Samuel 15:13-16,23).

Can you imagine the pain and sorrow David must have experienced and how he must have cried out to God? We don't have to speculate because David recorded his emotions and prayers in Psalm 3:1-6:

> *O Lord, how many are my foes!*
> *How many rise up against me!*
> *Many are saying of me,*
> *"God will not deliver him."*
>
> *But you are a shield around me, O Lord,*
> *You bestow glory on me and lift up my head.*
> *To the Lord I cry aloud,*
> *and he answers me from his holy hill.*
>
> *I lie down and sleep;*
> *I wake again, because the Lord sustains me.*
> *I will not fear the tens of thousands*
> *drawn up against me on every side.*

Much of David's history recorded in 1 and 2 Samuel, 1 Kings, and 1 Chronicles can be correlated to his great Psalms.

David kept a journal and, in so doing, kept strong his faith and spirit. What benefits might you derive from keeping a journal? Perhaps a journal will offer you:

- A way to preserve memories, now and forever;
- A means of expressing yourself;
- A stimulus to encouragement;
- A step toward greater awareness of God in your daily life;

- A record of aspirations and goals; a tracing of career development;
- An opportunity to enhance your writing skills;
- A means of reliving past pleasures and hard lessons.

Immediately when beginning your journal, you are faced with the matter of what to include. The simple answer is record what you wish. After all, it is your journal. Perhaps you will want to write about your attitudes and feelings, your hopes and fears, your dreams and fantasies, your crisis moments, your victories and defeats—anything of significance to you.

Set down the details about your personal interactions. Describe the persons, places, and events in your life. Spend time in reflection. You may want to include sketches or drawings if you have an artistic bent. Did you have an important conversation with someone? Write it out in dialogue form.

"How can I begin?" you may ask. Start with where you happen to be at this particular stage in your life. Or, write out a description of yourself and your present circumstances. If all else fails, set down the record of the day.

At what time of day will you do your journaling? Many people prefer late evening hours, just before bed, as they look back on the events of the last twenty-four hours. Others like the freshness of morning to review the previous day's happenings.

When and where you write may be determined somewhat by the method you select to make your record. Longhand? Computer? If you write in longhand, then you must decide on using individual sheets, a tablet, a bound notebook, or a loose-leaf notebook. The last possibility may tempt you at some future time to remove embarrassing entries. Plus, you are faced with decisions about a notebook's durability, size, and portability should you carry your journal outside your home.

Writing in longhand gives you opportunity to use different colors of ink to reflect your emotions of the moment. Happy? Green. Discouraged? Blue. Indifferent? Black. Angry? Red!

Must you feel obligated to write every day? Relax, you probably won't. Yet, this could be to your advantage. James Boswell, the famous biographer and journal writer of the 1700s, would sometimes procrastinate days, or even a week, before sitting down at his desk. Then he made each entry as if it were being recorded on the specific day indicated. This gave him the advantage of knowing in advance how something would come out. Yet, you would never guess this from reading his journal.

Regardless of when and in what form you write, you're going to be faced with the problem of privacy. How important is it to you that no one reads the innermost thoughts of your heart and soul? Again, you have several options. You can hide your journal or lock it up. You can write parts of it known only to yourself, as John Wesley did. (In this century, however, an enterprising fellow broke the famous evangelist's code and published his supposedly hidden-forever moments to a curious world.)

Another possibility is to do what one trusting wife and mother, who was undergoing several years of therapy, did. Since thoughts came into her mind during the middle of the night, she needed to keep the diary near her bed. At one point in her counseling, she called the family into her bedroom and pointed to a notebook she had placed on a nightstand. "This is my diary that I am keeping at my doctor's direction. I am trusting each of you, out of love and respect for me, to refrain from picking it up and reading it." So far as is known, no one violated her wishes.

Journal writing claims to be among the oldest and most important forms of personal writing.

Writing Autobiographies

> Everyone's life needs to be written, and it can best be told by the one who lives it.

Regardless of your age, the challenge and joys of writing your autobiography await you. Not only is your life important to you, but it has probably impacted the lives of others. Writing your life's story can be among the most valuable legacies you can give to your children and grandchildren. Successfully completing the challenge may delight you as few other accomplishments will.

"But nothing important has ever happened to me," you object. That's what you may think until you begin the task. However, you will likely be surprised as your personal history begins to unfold.

Consider how much you have witnessed or participated in during your lifetime. You've seen the world at war, the rise and fall of nations, the spectacular developments in electronic communications, the exploration of space, the spiritual apostasy of religious denominations, the devastation of new diseases, and the randomness of political terrorism.

You survived these events—maybe distantly, maybe heavily involved. In either case, now is the time to tell about it.

Writing autobiographies has become a significant hobby in this country. Many organizations will assist you in searching out your ancestry. Genealogists, both professional and amateur, offer guidance, as do librarians. Visit your local bookstore, and you may be amazed at the resources available to you.

Earlier in this chapter, you read suggested options for using longhand or a computer for writing your journal. The same applies for writing your autobiography.

All this may overwhelm you, but a simple way to begin your autobiography is to sketch out your personal timeline. Here's an example:

Age:	*Event:*
0	Born
4	Almost drowned
5	Started school
7	Flooded out
8	Moved to Iowa
9	Discovered opposite sex
9	Family broke up
9	Moved to Missouri
10	Born again!
14	Obtained first job
15	First fell in love
17	Graduated high school
18	Attended junior college
19	Became engaged
20	Left home

If sketching out your timeline horizontally is too much trouble, just list it vertically. Either way, you'll get a bird's-eye overview of your life. You can make your timeline as general or as specific as you wish. Instead of putting down your age at various points, perhaps you will want to indicate specific years.

Once you've laid a timeline foundation, you are ready to build your life's story on it. Here are some practical suggestions you may wish to follow.

Divide your life into various time segments, such as places you've lived, schools you've attended, family situations, personal relationships, triumphs, and tragedies. Or, divide your life into arbitrary five or ten year segments. You don't have to slavishly follow time periods consecutively. Plunge in at whatever time period you wish, perhaps with the one that holds the best and happiest memories.

Once you've chosen the period you wish to write about, make a list of your recollections, the significant people, your personal experiences pertaining to that time frame, and your appraisals and interpretations of what happened—both at the time you were passing through the events and from your present perspective. Now number all the entries in chronological order.

You're ready to write! It may be little more than a tentative first draft as you begin, but, as you write, additional details will come to mind. Unless you're facing a trip to the hospital or mortuary, proceed at a leisurely pace. If writing is really not your strong point, you could elect to jettison the writing approach and settle for an audio or video tape recorder to preserve your autobiography. However, tapes can be hard to edit.

After you've finished working with each specific period, you're ready to assemble all of them into a complete story. As you do this, you'll likely discover some events ought to be passed over entirely—for the sake of your own reputation or that of others.

You'll probably want to give your autobiography a title, a serious or humorous one. And now you're finished—temporarily. In His good providence, God may grant you future decades of experiences for you to add to your autobiography.

Topical Writing

> What do I think about a particular subject? I won't know until I write it out!

In addition to writing your journal and your autobiography, a third field of personal writing awaits. This concerns things that don't fall conveniently into either of the first two categories. For want of a better designation, call this topical writing. Identify, for example, an issue, a problem, a question, or a decision to make. Then write about it. Doing so will clarify your thoughts on the subject as nothing else can.

Try one or more of these topical writing assignments used by a college writing instructor:

1. *Your Own Psalm*

As you know, many of the psalms of David were written in response to the heavy things happening in his life. Have you gone through a difficult period recently? Then compose a psalm that may defuse your anger and yet be a source of praise to God. You may wish to compose your psalm in verse form in order to set it apart from your other writing.

2. *Infatuation or True Love*

Perhaps you or someone in your family currently has a love attraction that raises certain questions in your mind. You've given much thought about this internally, but what might you learn in addition by an objective appraisal?

Infatuation and true love, although sometimes possessing similarities, usually differ in significant ways. How can you tell the one from the other? Think about it, and then write out as many distinguishing characteristics as you can.

3. *Kinds of Worship*

If you have had the opportunity to visit different churches, you've observed that worship services can vary tremendously from one congregation and denomination to another. What do you imagine visitors think when they have an opportunity to visit your house of worship? Stop and analyze it.

Worship has been called the lost jewel in the Christian's crown. What kind of worship is offered to the Lord in the church services you attend? What, if anything, do you suggest as a means of recapturing what may have been lost?

4. *The Accounting*

In writing your journal and autobiography, the realization of how quickly time passes will likely come to your attention. As you go through the years of your life, perhaps words of Scripture come to mind: "And as it is appointed unto men once to die, but after this the judgment" (Hebrews 9:27 KJV). Writing about that certain prospect may better prepare you for it.

"And the secrets of his heart will be laid bare" (1 Corinthians 14:25). John Wesley wrote in the preface to his journal, "I shall shortly give account to him who is ready to judge the quick and the dead." Each of us will one day stand before the Lord. Does this prospect frighten you? Are you prepared for it? Why or why not?

5. *Dear Significant Other*

Sometimes writing about yourself can be extremely painful. Here's a writing assignment that you may not wish to tackle.

You usually post the letters you write, but you don't have to. You could write an unsent letter that could fill the void in communication and unblock feelings toward another person in your life. Take the most acute problem you have at this time. Write a letter to that person. Tell him or her what you haven't been able to express face-to-face.

One college coed responded with a three-page, single-spaced tirade to her father who had involved her in incest from the time she was five until she left home. "You bastard!" she wrote in part. "How could you have done this to me?"

6. *Medals of Honor*

Writing about various issues doesn't have to be all serious or threatening. It can be intriguing and fun. As an example, take a page from the past and write about something for which you should have received public recognition.

The military sometimes awards a Medal of Honor for heroism on the field of battle. Civilian awards are also given by civic and religious organizations in recognition of outstanding achievement. Think back on your life. What do you suppose you might be given a medal for? Indicate what that would be. Perhaps you will want to draft a citation that might be read at the time you receive your medal.

Journal writing. Autobiographical writing. Topical writing. These are just a few of the hundreds of topics you might like to write about in order to explore your feelings. So go to it! Unlike writing for publication, as mentioned earlier, your self-expression along these lines can be done with the freedom to write openly and honestly. Let that be your comfort and your challenge as you begin a lifelong journey of writing about yourself.

14 Poetry: Distillation of Life

by Jessica Shaver

I've done as many as eighty drafts of one poem.... I've found students shocked to learn that it can take me three years to finish a poem.

—Carolyn Forche

Just before Christmas one year, I was in a graduate poetry seminar in a state university when a soprano in a nearby classroom broke into a soaring aria from Handel's "Messiah": "For unto us a child is born, unto us a son is given—and His name shall be called Wonderful Counselor, Almighty God, the Everlasting Father, the Prince of Peace."

Lying before me was John Milton's poem, "On the Morning of Christ's Nativity," which begins:

> This is the Month, and this the happy morn
> Wherein the Son of Heav'n's eternal King,

Of wedded Maid, and Virgin Mother born,
Our great redemption from above did bring...

Wow! Try as the secularists might to keep Jesus Christ out of this university, He was right there in the classroom with us, permeating the very words we were reading, perfuming the air we were breathing!

How do Milton and Handel manage to penetrate to the very heart of a godless campus with the Gospel, when sermons, tracts, and personal witness usually meet with hostility, ridicule, or indifference? By mastering their craft.

If your craft is poetry, master it! Read great poetry. Take classes in literature, grammar, creative writing. Write. Join a critique group. Experiment with "technical tricks" like those below until you "revel in them," as Robert Frost did.

Rhyme

Rhyme works well when the tone of a poem is definite and assured, when you are making a statement, for example, about the faithfulness of Jesus Christ. It can strengthen the effectiveness of a dramatic or tension-building poem. Rhyme is not usually appropriate for poems that are searching, wondering, or struggling.

Be sure the rhyme sounds natural and what you are expressing benefits from a controlled, traditional form. If the reader senses that you have forced your language and grammar just to make the end of the line come out right, it will fit as painfully as Cinderella's glass slipper did on her stepsisters' feet.

Some famous poets use variations, such as half-rhyme (also known as imperfect, near, or slant rhyme) where vowel sounds don't match, as with love/leave. Emily Dickinson, Gerard Manley Hopkins, and William Butler Yeats were masters of half-rhyme. Alfred Lord Tennyson used assonance, where the sounds of the vowels match but the consonants don't, like half/bath or sweet/dreams. These variations are much harder to do well than you might think.

I find that an embryonic poem within me will determine its own form. Let the form reinforce the mood you want to capture.

Usually rhymes are at the end of lines. When words in the middle of two lines rhyme, it is called, understandably enough, internal rhyme.

"The Rime of the Ancient Mariner" by Samuel Taylor Coleridge, like other ballads, has lots of examples of internal rhyme:

> The fair breeze blew, the white foam flew,
> The furrow followed free;
> We were the first that ever burst
> Into that silent sea.

(Note also the alliteration—that is, the repetition of sounds, in this case f's and b's")

Meter

> But our love it was stronger by far than the love
> Of those who were older than we...
>
> from "Annabel Lee" by Edgar Allan Poe

Like songs, poems have different kinds of rhythm. They can have lines that are short and cheery, lines that are long and lilting, lines that are choppy and disturbing, or a combination. This rhythm, or meter, is a function of two things: the kind of beat (voice emphasis) and the number of beats per line.

Note the rhythm in the opening line of "Buick" by Karl Shapiro: "As a sloop with a sweep of immaculate wings on her delicate spine..." (As a SLOOP with a SWEEP of imMACulate WINGS on her DELicate SPINE...) Compare the number of beats in this line with the lines in the previously mentioned poem, "Annabel Lee," by Poe and in the following lines from "Bells," also by Poe:

> From the bells, bells, bells, bells,
> Bells, bells, bells—
> From the jingling and the tinkling of the bells.

Great poets, like great artists of all kinds, deliberately break the rules sometimes to get the effect they want. Here are the opening lines to John Donne's "Holy Sonnet XIV":

> Batter my heart, three-personed God; for you
> As yet but knock, breathe, shine, and seek to mend.

If Donne had used a consistent sonnet meter, the "beat" of each line would be on every second syllable. Instead, he opens with "BATter my heart..." The beat or stress is on the very first syllable. Why? Donne's choice was deliberate. He wanted his readers not only to hear a word meaning "to hit" but also to feel the impact of his passion: Lord, You're kind and loving to me but that's not enough to overcome my tendency to stray! I want so much to obey you, but I'm weak. Force yourself on me! Make me obey!

What you want to say in a poem can be underscored—or undermined—by the meter with which you say it. Back in 1661, a young Puritan named Michael Wigglesworth wrote "a poetical description of the Great and Last Judgment" called "The Day of Doom." Modern critics claim his meter is inappropriate to his solemn subject:

> Earth's dwellers all, both great and small,
>   have wrought iniquity,
> And suffer must, for it is just,
>   eternal misery.

What do you think? Does this rhythm (and internal rhyme) reinforce the idea of misery—or does it sound playful: "What, lost your mittens? You naughty kittens!"

If we use meter at all, we want it to echo and enhance what we are trying to convey.

Blank Verse

> She ran on tiptoe down the darkened passage
> To meet him in the doorway with the news
> And put him on his guard. "Silas is back."
>
> "Death of the Hired Man" by Robert Frost

Before rhyme became popular in English verse (in the late fourteenth century), many poets used something called blank verse. Blank verse has, instead of rhyme, a regular meter or beat to it. The particular meter used in blank verse is iambic pentameter, that is, ten syllables per line, with stress on every second one.

Don't let the unfamiliar term dismay you. Remember it's how we speak, the normal way we emphasize our words. To prove it, take a look at the sentence I just wrote. It could be written as three iambic pentameter lines:

Don't LET the UNfamMIliar TERM disMAY
you, JUST reMEMber THAT it's HOW we SPEAK,
the NORmal WAY we EMphaSIZE our WORDS.

If you experiment a bit, you'll see that iambic pentameter is a comfortable way of reading. Poems in this form can go for pages, like a horse cantering, without tiring the reader (rider). With the variation of an extra beat on the word "passage," Frost's previously mentioned poem is a perfect example. Notice how natural the stresses are, just like conversation. Much of the finest verse in English—by Shakespeare, Milton, Wordsworth, Tennyson, and Wallace Stevens—is in blank verse.

Here are two other examples of iambic pentameter: "I should have been a pair of ragged claws..." (T.S. Eliot); "And doom'd to death, though fated not to die" (John Dryden).

Free Verse

Free verse has been compared to playing tennis without a net. It has no set pattern or structure. Line length can be irregular, and rhyme, if used at all, can be more or less random. William Blake and Goethe wrote some free verse, but it really became popular with Walt Whitman and has now nearly eclipsed rhymed verse, except on greeting cards.

Here are examples of how varied the form can be:

When I heard the learn'd astronomer,
When the proofs, the figures, were ranged in columns before
 me,
When I was shown the charts and diagrams, to add, divide,
 and measure them,
When I sitting heard the astronomer where he lectured with
 much applause in the lecture-room,
How soon unaccountable I became tired and sick,
Till rising and gliding out I wander'd off by myself,

In the mystical moist night-air, and from time to time,
Look'd up in perfect silence at the stars.
"When I Heard the Learn'd Astronomer" by Walt Whitman

I follow
the seam of light
stitched
by my mothers,
Eve's grief
flows unbroken
into Elizabeth's joy.

"Mary's Song" by Katherine Meyer

Narrative, Dramatic, and Lyric Poetry

Let's look at the three major categories of poetry: narrative, dramatic, and lyric.

Narrative poems, such as ballads and epics, tell a story. Ballads were originally folk songs about tragic events or local legends. They're full of action and dialogue so they're easy to commit to memory. Most ballads are written in quatrains (four-line stanzas), with the second and fourth lines rhyming. Sometimes stanzas are repeated as refrains. "The Yarn of the Nancy Bell" by William Schwenck Gilbert is a humorous ballad about a shipwrecked crew resorting to cannibalism:

...Then only the cook and me was left,
And the delicate question, "Which
Of us goes to the kettle?" arose,
And we argued it out as sich...

And he stirred it round and round and round,
And he sniffed at the foaming froth;
When I ups with his heels, and smothers his squeals
In the scum of the boiling broth...

Narrative epics celebrate the exploits of superhuman heroes. Book-length epics include Homer's *Iliad and Odyssey*, Virgil's *Aeneid*, Milton's *Paradise Lost*, as well as the Anglo-Saxon poem *Beowulf* and the *Babylonian Gilgamesh*.

Unlike narrative poems, dramatic poems don't give third-person accounts of someone else. They become the "someone else," speaking in the voice of an historical or fictional character.

For instance, in this bit from the dramatic poem, "Ulysses," Alfred Lord Tennyson expresses what Ulysses might have felt as an old man, remembering past adventures when he was restless in his retirement:

> How dull it is to pause, to make an end,
> To rust unburnished, not to shine in use!
> ...Come, my friends,
> 'Tis not too late to seek a newer world.
> Push off, and sitting well in order smite
> The sounding furrows; for my purpose holds
> To sail beyond the sunset, and the baths
> Of all the western stars, until I die.

Did you notice that it is written in blank verse?

Poems that are neither narrative nor dramatic are usually lyric. Lyric poems are shorter and can be composed in almost any meter on almost any subject, and they are by far the most common poetry written today. Rather than telling a story, they capture a feeling or a mood, like "Half Moon" by Federico Garcia Lorca (translation by W.S. Merwin) :

> The moon goes over the water.
> How tranquil the sky is!
> She goes scything slowly
> the old shimmer from the river;
> meanwhile a young frog
> takes her for a little mirror.

You might say that lyric poetry is less concerned with a process over time than with a point in time. Also, rather than describing emotion, the poet attempts to evoke it—to recreate in the reader an emotion he felt.

Lyric poetry includes sonnets, like this thought-provoking one by John Keats:

When I have fears that I may cease to be
Before my pen has glean'd my teeming brain,
Before high piled books, in charactry,
Hold like rich garners the full ripen'd grain;
When I behold, upon the night's starr'd face,
Huge cloudy symbols of a high romance,
And think that I may never live to trace
Their shadows, with the magic hand of chance;
And when I feel, fair creature of an hour,
That I shall never look upon thee more,
Never have relish in the fairy power
Of unreflecting love;—then on the shore
Of the wide world I stand alone, and think
Till love and fame to nothingness do sink.

"When I Have Fears That I May Cease to Be"

The sonnet form is exacting: fourteen lines, each iambic pentameter, grouped into quatrains, or four-line units. Writing them is good discipline, and reading a great sonnet is rewarding. A good one will yield richness to anyone who invests the time and effort to read it several times.

Three quatrains and a rhyming couplet form the traditional English or Shakespearean sonnet. The Italian or Petrarchian sonnet is composed of two quatrains with a sestet, that is, six lines with their own separate rhyme pattern.

Every good sonnet has a "turn" or counterthrust, something that adds a new dimension to the quatrains or takes them in a different direction. In the English sonnet, the turn comes in the couplet. Look at the previous example again. For twelve lines, Keats is lamenting that his early death is going to deprive him of a chance to write all that he wants to write and to experience romance. But in the last two and a half lines, he trips us up with a refreshingly unexpected conclusion: In the light of eternity, fame and love fade into insignificance. His thought here reminds me of two lines of a hymn: "And the things of earth will grow strangely dim/In the light of His glory and grace." What a message!

The turn in the Italian sonnet, as you might expect, comes in the last six lines.

Another lyric form is the haiku (HAH-ee-koo):

Old pond
Frog jumps—
Kerplop!

Basho

Like the famous poem above (translated here by my brother Ted Reynolds), haiku are poems that are simple in form, yet evocative in content. Developed in sixteenth century Japan, they paint a mental picture of some natural object or scene, which stirs in the reader's emotions, memories, and/or reflections. They are sense experiences (sound, sight, taste, touch, smell) bottled in words. Ideally, they are supposed to have at least an implied seasonal reference, but they don't always.

Instead of using rhyme or meter, haiku are normally seventeen syllables arranged in three lines of five, seven, and five syllables. The third line is often like a punch line, an eye-opener. It may spark awe, surprise, mystery, delight, nostalgia—whatever the author desires.

Here is one of my favorites, written by my brother Ted during the '60s:

How can I believe
This soft rain that I so love—
Radioactive?

One of my brother Tim's:

Kill! Kill! Kill! Kill! Swifts
wing tip to wing tip, insect
Armageddon, dusk.

And one of mine:

Omnipresent God
contained in all His fullness
within this zygote.

You can see how broad a category lyric poetry is, in that it includes both sonnets and haiku!

Countermotion

The old dog barks backward without getting up.
I can remember when he was a pup.

"The Span of Life" by Robert Frost

Look at this poem by Robert Frost. That's the whole thing: just two lines. Can "the span of life" be summed up in two lines? *These* two lines?

Think of the contrast between a young dog and an old one. Certainly one difference between them is energy level. A puppy is active, bouncy—always ready to play. An old dog saves his strength for getting to his dinner bowl or protecting his turf. In line 1, Frost uses this single characteristic to summarize all of old age (doing this is called synecdoche). The old dog doesn't even bother to challenge strangers anymore. He has rheumatism, or it's too much trouble. He just turns his head and goes through the motions.

Separately, lines 1 and 2 are merely observations about an animal. Together, however, the contrast between the two arouses a series of ripples or overtones about the brevity of all life.

In my favorite book about poetry, *How Does a Poem Mean?*, authors John Ciardi and Miller Williams call this countermotion. The two lines of Frost's poem are like a seesaw in balance, with a fulcrum causing a pause and a change between them. The tone changes: The first line is objective; the second is nostalgic. The pace changes: The first is brisk; the second is slower and more reflective. We've already discussed countermotion in sonnets.

Succinctness

Poetry is to creative writing what a telegram is to a letter. (If it seems to ramble, it should do so for a purpose.) Every word has to be necessary, every line under control. Anybody can write. What makes a *good* writer is *rewriting*. This applies as much to poetry as to any other genre: Getting it on paper is only the first step. Evaluate the whole. Does it make the point you want to achieve? Could it make the point better? Have more punch? Evaluate the parts. If you were spending a dollar a word to send this "telegram," what words would you cut? What one word could you substitute where you've used several? What active verb could you substitute for a passive one, which single adjective for two or three?

Self-edit. Be terse, succinct. Groom your work. Use synecdoches to hint at the whole of something. In "September 1913," William Butler Yeats conveyed his attitude toward the whole merchant class of Ireland by referring to the "greasy till." In his nostalgic "He Remembers Forgotten Beauty," Yeats speaks of "the murderous moth." Even if you haven't read the rest of the poem, can't you guess what Yeats might be saying about life?

Restrictions (structure, deadlines, word counts) imposed by the form itself or by an editor can actually help by forcing you to condense, to say it more concisely. Distillation only throws the point you are trying to make into sharper focus.

Ambiguity

Farewell, thou child of my right hand, and joy;
My sin was too much hope of thee, loved boy…

"On My First Son" by Ben Jonson

In post-war Japan, soldiers' widows made a living as best they could. One woman converted the second floor of her small home to accommodate a small seamstress business and hung a sign in her window: "Ladies have fits upstairs."

Ambiguity. Is it a nuisance that hinders understanding, an accident that creates absurdities, or a tool to exploit multiple possibilities in order to evoke appreciation on multiple levels? Or, all of the above?

To the lawyer, the legislator, or the real estate investment broker, ambiguity is irritating. It leaves documents that need to be explicit open to misinterpretation. If your secretary tells you, "You have no business meeting today," you don't want to be guessing whether she's giving you information about your day's schedule or passing a moral judgment on some personal rendezvous.

However, in a poem, clarity is not necessarily the overriding goal. Like an Oriental brush painting, it's intriguing to suggest what you can't see with an unfinished stroke or a wisp of mist. If two or more possible meanings fit the context, you can even work them counter punctually, with one playing against the other or supplying depth or overtones.

The first line of Keats' "Ode on a Grecian Urn" is "Thou still unravish'd bride of quietness." Does "still" mean "yet" or "immobile" or both? I would suggest to you that Keats deliberately chose a word that conveyed both ideas.

John Ciardi calls ambiguity "the exploitation of a word's two or more meanings…an 'under-meaning.'" Sometimes these two meanings support and reinforce each other. Sometimes they enhance each other with additional nuances. Other times they clash with each other, pointing out a paradox.

Dylan Thomas used ambiguity even in the title of his poem to his father, "Do Not Go Gentle into That Good Night." In the term "good night," he captures the finality of death and makes an ironic comment on it.

Take a look at Ben Jonson's deeply felt poem, previously mentioned. Jonson lived at the dawn of the seventeenth century. In 1603, his seven-year old son, Ben Jr., died of the plague, and the brokenhearted father wrote him this poem beginning, "Farewell, child of my right hand…" (the literal meaning of "Benjamin"). Does the first line—"Farewell, thou child of my right hand, and joy"—mean "Farewell, child who was my joy" or "Farewell, child, and farewell, joy?" Both work, in this context. There is also a play on the word "farewell," meaning goodbye, and the wish from which it is derived: "fare well," in this case, fare well in eternity.

Experiment with ambiguity to give your poetry depth.

Voice

As with other genres of literature, you don't have to be yourself when you write poetry. You can climb inside someone else's mind and heart. For instance, when Tennyson wrote in his poem "Ulysses," "Matched with an aged wife, I mete and dole/Unequal laws unto a savage race…" you wouldn't know he is really a twenty-four-year-old Cambridge dropout. He has become the Greek hero. In "The Lady of Shalott," on the other hand, he speaks as a lovelorn maiden.

Lots of children's poetry is written in a child's voice. A.A. Milne sometimes wrote from the viewpoint of his young son, Christopher Robin: "But now I am six, I'm as clever as clever,/ So I think I'll be six now for ever and ever." (I had to recite this poem once, and I have never lived down the humiliation—because I was *seven*!)

A.A. Milne might even be Christopher Robin being someone else: "I'm a great big lion in my cage,/And I often frighten Nanny with a roar..."

Someday, if you haven't already, you'll write something that feels comfortable, that's really uniquely *you*. It's usually something that grows out of a process of maturing and improving your technique. That's your voice as a poet.

Mood

Words, chosen for their meaning, their sound, or both, can set a mood. If you want a wistful, melancholy mood, choose words that evoke images like T.S. Eliot's in "The Love Song of J. Alfred Prufrock": "I have measured out my life with coffee spoons..."

How about suspense? In "The Pirates of Penzance," Gilbert and Sullivan choose monosyllabic words with staccato sounds. Reading them mimics the precise tread of pirates creeping into sleeping households:

> With cat-like tread,
> Upon our prey we steal,
> In silence dread
> Our cautious way we feel...

There's no better example of how you can change the mood of a poem than Edgar Allan Poe's "Bells." In four stanzas, he takes us from sleigh bells "jingling and tinkling," to wedding bells "rhyming and chiming," to alarm bells "twanging and clanging," to iron bells "moaning and groaning." Poe uses words with similar sounds (alliteration)—blunt t's, sharp-edged k's, or lilting mellow l's and smooth s's. He chooses words that imitate their meaning (onomatopoeia), like "tinkle," "gush," and "shriek."

What is the mood of this final stanza from "Little Orphant Annie," by James Whitcomb Riley? How does he create this mood?

Look for alliteration and onomatopoeia:

An' Little Orphant Annie says when the blaze is blue,
An' the lamp-wick sputters, an' the wind goes *woo-oo!*
An' you hear the crickets quit, an' the moon is gray,
An' the lightnin'-bugs in dew is all squenched away...
You better mind yer parents, an' yer teachers fond an' dear,
An' churish them 'at loves you, an' dry the orphant's tear,
An' he'p the pore an' needy ones 'at clusters all about,
Er the Gobble-uns'll git you
    Ef you
        Don't
            Watch
                Out!

Imagery

Here lies resting, out of breath,
Out of turns, Elizabeth
Whose quicksilver toes not quite
Cleared the whirring edge of night.

Earth whose circles round us skim
Till they catch the lightest limb,
Shelter now Elizabeth
And for her sake trip up Death.
"Little Elegy for a Child Who Skipped Rope" by X.J. Kennedy

Isn't that beautifully expressed? This is a poem that *works,* as they say, because of its consistent imagery. Kennedy chose appropriate picture language to describe the death of a little girl. He used "out of breath" and "out of turns" as synonyms for being dead and the analogy of a moving jump rope, as in "whirring edge of night" and "circles round us skim" to describe death itself. Elizabeth's toes didn't quite clear (evade) death, and neither will those of the most agile of us, for it "catches the lightest limb." There are double meanings (overtones) throughout the poem.

The second stanza is a prayer, in a form that goes back to the Greeks and the Romans, for the earth to shelter her. Kennedy adds, "and for her sake trip up Death." This phrase actually does what it means. It deliberately trips you up as you read it.

Emily Dickinson was a master of imagery. I hope you are familiar with her poem "A Narrow Fellow in the Grass." She refers to the subject of the poem as "a narrow fellow in the grass," "a spotted shaft," "a whip lash unbraiding in the sun," one of "nature's people," but she never tells you outright what she is writing about. She doesn't need to. What else "divides grass as with a comb," "wrinkles and is gone"? What else causes "tighter breathing,/And Zero at the Bone." (Zero what, by the way? Does it matter?)

"His notice sudden is." How do these words convey aural as well as visual imagery?

Images can include an oxymoron, like Dickinson's "blue, uncertain, stumbling buzz" in "I Heard a Fly Buzz When I Died."

Imagery makes what you write fresh and original. It can give a tired and overworked idea a whole new look. Imagery may be what makes poetry poetry. Poems may or may not rhyme, may be short or long, may be highly structured and formal or rambling, but something in them must project the imagination beyond the poem itself. Above all, poetry must be an observation with universal echoes, a personal revelation from one heart that reverberates in another, creating pleasure and intimacy.

Making the Transition from Articles to Books

15

by Dennis E. Hensley

I am convinced that all writers are optimists whether they concede the point or not.... How otherwise could any human being sit down to a pile of blank sheets and decide to write, say two hundred thousand words on a given theme.

—Thomas Costain

By the time I was thirty, I had written a thousand freelance articles for every sort of periodical imaginable: *Reader's Digest, People, The Baptist Bulletin, The Detroit Free Press, The War Cry, Stereo, Florida Real Estate Professional's Journal, Grit, Essence, Plus 60 Magazine,* and *The Christian Reader.* If it had a page of "Writer's Guidelines," I had probably cracked a byline in it.

However, I had never given much thought to writing a book until I received a call from Bill Willard, an editor with the business books division of Bobbs-Merrill Publishers.

"I was flying to Indianapolis this past Monday," Bill told me, "and I happened to read the article you wrote on time management for

Piedmont Airline's in-flight magazine, *Pace*. It was terrific. I'm interested in having you write an entire book on time management for my publishing house. Could you do a 35,000-word trade paperback for us? I'd like to have it on the market by this time next year. Are you interested?"

I was stunned.

"I, uh, write articles, not books," I stammered. "I've never written anything longer than a 2,500 word feature."

"That'll work just fine," said Bill, not losing a bit of his enthusiasm for the book project. "We own a magazine called *Market Builder*. It's for sales executives. I want you to write twelve different features on aspects of time management—things like time management while on the phone, while at the office, when traveling, and so on. Make each feature about 2,000 to 2,500 words long. We'll run them as a monthly column for one year in our magazine, then we'll have you combine all the columns into a book. You can add some sidebars, graphics, reading lists, a table of contents, and an index. Then we'll be in business. How about four hundred dollars per column and then a five-thousand-dollar advance for the book? Do we have a deal?"

Two minutes after I hung up the phone, I was in the book writing business. A year later my book, *Staying Ahead of Time*, was released on Bobbs-Merrill's business books imprint (R & R Newkirk). Since then, I've written twenty-seven books for such publishers as Harper Collins, Thomas Nelson Publishers, Harvest House Publishers, Servant Publishing, Warner Press, Broadman & Holman Publishers, Pacific Press, and Poetica Press. For at least fourteen of these books, I've used the same system of creating a series of articles first and then turning them into a book. Here's how it works.

Step One: Look for a Multi-Faceted Topic

Select something you can write about from many different perspectives and for a wide variety of readers. For my first book, time management was a perfect topic. It could be approached from a personal and a business standpoint. Plus, it could be of value to people of all ages and in all walks of life. There were sections on time management for parents, students, managers, employees, salespeople, entrepreneurs, and executives. The topics focused on included time management in offices, cars, airports, at home, at school, and even while on vacation. The range of subjects was vast.

This same principle applies when writing books strictly for Christian reading audiences. My book, *The Jesus Effect* (Pacific Press), was a book that drew examples from the New Testament of how Jesus dealt with a wide variety of human characteristics, such as love, endurance, boldness, success, composure, and discipline. The book covered fifteen chapters of different topics. Within each chapter, there were subtopics. This is the key: To find an umbrella topic under which you can expound on numerous related subcategories. After all, if you are going to write a book, you are going to need enough material.

Step Two: Prepare an Extensive Outline of Your Book

A good nonfiction book will have chapters on the background of its subject; the current theories, case histories, and research related to it; interviews with several experts in the field; reports on innovations, experiments, and new concepts; and notes on any variations on a theme.

You'll need to determine in advance where you'll want to place all this material in the chapters of your book, how detailed each chapter will need to be, and whether or not the chapters will have sidebars, quizzes, suggested reading lists, and other ancillary inserts. You'll also need to decide whether (and where) you will need to support your written text with photographs, maps, cartoons, charts, graphs, diagrams, and other visual materials. Having done all this, you will then have a blueprint from which to work.

Step Three: Focus on Specific Themes

Write from a narrow focus. For example, I planned to have a chapter in *Staying Ahead of Time* called, "Time Management While Traveling." I broke that broad topic into seven categories: subways, automobiles, trains, ships, buses, taxis, and airplanes.

Each subcategory was then divided into problem solving procedures, which I explained in separate freelance articles. For the airplane section, for instance, I wrote a freelance piece called, "Overcoming Terminal Problems," which explained ten useful things a traveler could accomplish while stuck in a terminal during a long layover. I used that as part of one of the *Market Builder* columns and later freelanced it to *Roto, Gulfshore Life, Fort Wayne Today Magazine,* and nine other periodicals.

You, likewise, should attempt to gain as many freelance sales at this point as possible. You'll be doing this for two reasons: to generate cash flow while writing your book and to stack up byline credits, which will later prove to a publisher that you are a recognized "authority" in your field. Credibility is vitally important in book publishing.

Step Four: Prepare Folders on the Various Topics

Take manila folders and label them by the chapter titles. File published versions of your articles related to each chapter subcategory. Save copies of your research and unused notes, too, so that this additional material can be used later for anecdotal fillers, sidebars, and transition stories when you actually write the chapters. You can't just jam articles together and call them a chapter. Each chapter needs to flow smoothly from one topic to the next.

Step Five: Write the Book's Chapters

After you've developed each subcategory by as many freelance articles and/or columns as possible, combine your material into chapters. Add more quotations than you did in your articles. Cite more references and use footnotes, if appropriate. Decide where to insert photographs and other graphics. Prepare everything in a neatly typed manuscript format.

Step Six: Sell the Book Manuscript

Prepare a book proposal. Include your book's table of contents with a brief synopsis of each chapter, two completed sample chapters of the book (not necessarily the first two), and a cover letter that hits hard on your expertise and the wide reader interest in the subject matter. This can be established by enclosing tear sheets of your published articles from at least a dozen periodicals.

Enclose a self-addressed, stamped envelope (SASE) with each submission. Keep submitting your proposal until someone asks to see the entire manuscript, then offers you a contract for it.

Step Seven: Sell Excerpts from the Book

After your book is published, send copies to editors for whom you have written articles and ask for help in exposing the book to the public.

I did this with *Staying Ahead of Time*. Audrey Edwards, then editor of *Essence*, bought excerpt rights to Chapter Two of the book and ran it as an article. John Brady, then editor of *Writer's Digest*, bought excerpt rights to part of Chapter Three and ran it as a sidebar to a cover story he was doing on time management for writers.

All tallied, eleven editors bought excerpts, and six others opted to write reviews of the book. This not only gave me cash flow from the excerpt sales, which were split 50/50 with the book publisher, but also helped boost nationwide sales of the book.

Step Eight: Develop a Spin-Off Topic

While your first book is selling well, use that momentum to land your next book contract. Develop an idea for a sequel or a companion volume on a related topic. Now that you are a published author, your credibility will be established. Capitalize on that while it's hot.

I sent Bobbs-Merrill a proposal for a book called *Positive Workaholism*, which combined concepts of time management with systems of personal motivation. The publishers accepted it, and the public bought it like crazy. It sold four times as many copies as *Staying Ahead of Time*. It was excerpted in *Success!* magazine and was eventually developed into an audiocassette album by Success Motivation, Inc., of Waco, Texas. All this from a guy who once said, "I write articles, not books."

The process then starts over. Some people ask me if they should send out six or eight copies of the book proposal to that many different publishers at the same time. Personally, I don't recommend that because if two or more come back wanting the book, you will have to disappoint someone. That burns a bridge of trust you might have built between you and that publisher. If you are that gung-ho to do multiple marketing, let me suggest that you get a literary agent to do multiple submissions of your book proposal. They can get away with that sort of thing. Better yet, come up with four or five different proposals for different books and send them out simultaneously. Whichever book idea clicks with a publisher, that's the one you will concentrate on finishing and selling.

16 The Power of Your Story: Written or Spoken

by Marlene Bagnull

I take the view, and always have, that if you cannot say what you are going to say in twenty minutes you ought to go away and write a book about it.

—Lord Brabazon

There was a man who had two sons. The younger one said to his father, 'Father, give me my share of the estate...'" In essence: "I want what's coming to me now!"

So begins one of Jesus' most remembered and loved stories, recorded for us in Luke 15:11-32. We remember it because it speaks to us. We love it because it gives us hope whether we're a parent waiting for a prodigal to come home, a prodigal who wonders if he will be welcomed home, or the older brother (or sister) who feels unappreciated and unloved.

Jesus frequently told stories because he knew it was one of the best ways he could connect with people. I believe he is telling us to "go and do likewise."

How can we effectively harness the power of the story to reach our listeners and readers? By telling and writing the stories we know best—our own personal stories of how we came to know Christ and the difference He is making in our lives.

Maybe it's because I really don't enjoy research, or maybe it's because, as my mentor has frequently told me, I have so much grist (problems) for my writing and speaking mill. Whatever the reason, almost from the beginning of my writing and speaking ministry, I've drawn on my personal experiences. Not only am I convinced that it's one of the most powerful ways to minister to others, it's also a way I can live out the "all things work together for good" promise. You see, if even one person is helped through my experience, my struggle has not been in vain and the evil one is not the victor.

Now please don't misunderstand what I'm saying. I don't like problems! The truth is, I'd much rather run from problems than face them, but running usually isn't an option. It doesn't help that problems are groupies. Seriously, when was the last time you had only *one* problem you needed to solve? Problems rarely come singly. Instead, they seem to gang up on us until we feel surrounded and overwhelmed.

"Why, God?" is a question people frequently ask. But Jesus never promised us a problem-free life. What He has promised is always to be with us. That's the message people need to hear, and that's the message we have the privilege of sharing as writers and speakers. But how can we share it effectively? How can we harness the power of the story?

Keep a Journal

Although we are convinced that we'll *never* forget the details of what happened or the intensity of our feelings, we will! Time is a wonderful healer of memories. We also seem to have a propensity for remembering the wrong things and forgetting what we need to remember. I call it the "I'd Rather Go Back to Egypt" syndrome. Parents who are hoarse from repeating themselves, call it selective listening/remembering.

What's the remedy? Keep a journal! Not a journal that becomes a ball and chain that creates all sorts of guilt when you don't write in it, but a journal that is used to capture the lessons God is teaching you so you don't forget them—and don't need to repeat them over and over!

Journaling will help you "write from the heart as well as from the head," Luci Shaw said in *Lifepath*.

If journaling isn't for you, write letters and keep copies. Confiding in people on paper is a wonderful way to work through problems. Email makes it even easier to write and save your thoughts. Set your system to automatically save what you send and sort it into folders according to subject. When the time comes to write and speak on a problem you've faced and overcome, you'll have a wealth of material to draw from.

Inventory and Reflect on Your Life Experiences

Some experiences are best not shared. Let's face it. Our listeners and readers really aren't interested in all the boring details of our lives. Nor are they likely to be interested in our family tree. But I guarantee they will be interested in the times God lifted us "out of the slimy pit, out of the mud and mire" and set our feet "on a rock" and gave us "a firm place to stand" (Psalm 40:2). When we sing that new song of praise to him, "many will see and fear and put their trust in the Lord" (Psalm 40:3).

One important principle—don't tell or write it too soon. When we're still in the midst, it's best to share our experiences only with our journal and a couple of close friends—not an audience of strangers. Our readers and listeners want to be able to look to us for answers—answers we can't give them if we're still stuck in the mud.

Does that mean we have to totally work through a problem and be walking in complete victory before we speak or write about it? I'm sure that's what the adversary wants us to believe, for if that were the case, groups would never be able to find speakers, and there would be few books in print. But have we gotten far enough on the other side of the problem to have gained some perspective? If we're still trying to gain a toehold to climb out of the pit, we can't pull anyone else out.

One experience all Christians need to be prepared to share is our salvation testimony. But perhaps you grew up in a Christian home, always went to Sunday school and church, and can't remember a time when you didn't believe. Does that mean you don't have a testimony to share? Of course not!

Although you may not have a dramatic testimony of how God saved you, no doubt you do have many stories of things God has been teaching you throughout your life journey. These stories may have a far greater impact on the believer who is struggling to live out his or her faith in the midst of the daily grind.

Let's face it. The real testing ground for our faith is in the events of everyday life. We know we need the Lord when big problems hit, but all too often we may try to handle on our own the little things that catch us off guard or try our patience. For instance, how many of us have no business advertising we're a Christian on the bumper stickers of our cars when we are anything but a positive witness behind the wheel?

Check Your Heart

"We can be mirrors that brightly reflect the glory of the Lord," the apostle Paul says in 2 Corinthians 3:18 (TLB). We need to ask ourselves if that is, indeed, our goal when we pick up our pen or stand up to speak. Remember that both our arms (and our readers and listeners) will get bent out of shape if we're intent on patting ourselves on the back. Our goal needs to be to point the readers to God, not to ourselves.

Humility is not only a virtue, it's a necessity for writers and speakers. "Do not exalt yourself or set yourself up as the perfect example of truth in action.... Remember, that your reader cannot identify with, or take advice from, a know-it-all," Ethel Herr says in the excellent book *An Introduction to Christian Writing* (ACW Press).

"And all of you serve each other with humble spirits," the apostle Peter advises, "for God gives special blessings to those who are humble, but sets himself against those who are proud" (1 Peter 5:5 TLB). What a terrifying thing it would be to have God set himself against us! We dare not let our press releases go to our head.

While we can fool men, we can never fool God. He knows the motives of our hearts. May we never forget that our Lord didn't come to be served, but to serve others. If we want to one day hear him say, "Well done, good and faithful servant" (Matthew 25:23), fame and fortune cannot be our goal.

Know Your Audience

Taking the time to find out as much as you can about your audience is one of the best ways to make certain your story will speak to their needs. What is their average age? Are they single, married, or divorced? Do they have children and, if so, are their children infants or toddlers, school age, or grown? Is your audience both male and female? Are they primarily high school or college graduates, professional or blue collar? And, so as not to unwittingly step on toes, if you're speaking to a church group or writing for a denominational magazine, what are their basic tenets of faith? Can you speak or write to them without feeling compelled to try and change their beliefs?

The business world spends thousands of dollars on market research before developing and releasing a new product. Shouldn't we at least spend some time in researching our audience? Once we identify who we are "targeting," we can take better "aim" by praying for them and seeking the Lord for the message He would have us bring to them.

Have a Clear Focus

Have you ever gotten behind the wheel of your car, driven a couple of blocks from home, and suddenly realized you don't have a clue where you're going? It's really embarrassing when you have someone with you and need to ask your passenger!

We all lead busy lives and have lots of things pressing in on us. It's so easy for our thinking to get muddled, and that's *not* a good thing for a writer or speaker. If we don't know where we're going in the message or manuscript we're preparing, how will we ever get there?

Years ago Lee Roddy taught me the importance of a one-sentence focus statement. Because Lee knows how wordy I can be, he eliminated my commas and semi-colons. (Since then I've put some of my "gems" on overheads and challenged the participants in my writers' seminars to diagram my sentence.)

Part of our problem is that we tend to want to tell or write too much on any one given topic. While I believe in the importance of providing real content, I also know that I can easily lose my reader or listener if I give too much detail.

Resist the temptation to fall in love with your words. Writers and speakers need to be ruthless, eliminating words, phrases, sentences, and entire paragraphs (sometimes even entire points in a speaking outline) that do not fall under your focus statement and do not further your purpose for the message you're seeking to present.

Create Reader/Listener Identification

It's all too easy for a reader to put down our book or a listener to tune us out. How do we create reader/listener identification to prevent that from happening? We've got to "get real." That means we need to take off our mask and be open, honest, and vulnerable.

"I don't understand myself," the apostle Paul admitted. "I don't know why I do the things I do, and why I don't do the things I want to do" (see Romans 7:15-19). If one of the leaders of the early church and the writer of a third of the New Testament could admit his struggles, why can't we?

"I don't mean to say I am perfect. I haven't learned all I should even yet," Paul confessed to the Christians in Philippi (Philippians 3:12 TLB).

It's so important to communicate this to our readers and listeners. If they think that we think we've "arrived" and that we're talking down to them, they're going to look for ways to trip us up and prove us wrong. But if we're willing to admit that we've made mistakes, we're likely to win a friend who will want to listen to what we have to say.

Master the Craft

A story has a beginning, a middle, and an end. Without these elements, you have an anecdote, not a story.

Your beginning has to immediately capture your reader or listener's attention. This is best done by presenting the problem with no apparent solution. Then develop your story by showing how things went from bad to worse. By the time you reach the crisis point, your audience should be sitting on the edge of their seats. This is the "you can hear a pin drop" or the "can't put the book down" moment. Please don't spoil it by presenting a "I came to realize" solution. Although the turning point may begin with an "ah-ha" moment, *something* needs to happen. And that big something is *change.*

Have you ever watched a movie only to feel cheated at the end because there really wasn't any change in the situation? Instead, you were left up in the air wondering what happened. Don't cheat your readers or listeners by not tying up the loose ends at the end of your story.

Mastering the craft includes learning how to pace your story and how to write and speak with such excellence that the readers or listeners don't have to work to follow the storyline. Instead, the master craftsman learns to so draw them into the story that they don't hear the clock ticking and don't want the story to end.

Provide a Strong Take-away

Your take-away is the answer to the "What difference does this make?" question. While stories can be told and written simply to entertain, as followers of the Lord Jesus Christ,our stories need to serve the far greater purpose of introducing people to Him or encouraging them to grow in Him. That doesn't mean our stories need to have a "now I lived happily ever after" ending. I've always resisted singing the chorus of that old hymn that proclaims, "Now I am happy all day long." It seems sing-songy and pat, and I don't think our readers and listeners will buy it. Sometimes life is really, really hard, and bad things do happen to good people. But we can show them that God is our strength, our peace, and our joy despite what life throws at us. Sometimes the greatest miracle and our strongest testimony is of God's grace to help us hold on and work through the problem. A miraculous removal of the problem does not help us grow.

Are You Ready?

Writing and speaking from life experience—sharing *your* story, your testimony, of God's working in your life—is certainly not the easiest form of writing or speaking. You can expect to get put to the test by the evil one. He will try and discredit your message, so be on guard."Put on all of God's armor so that you will be able to stand safe against all strategies and tricks of Satan," the apostle Paul counsels (Ephesians 6:11 TLB).

You may face criticism and even persecution by people who don't want to hear what you have to say. Jesus did! "Since they persecuted me, naturally they will persecute you," he said (John 15:20 TLB) But he also said, "When you are reviled and persecuted and lied about because you are my followers—wonderful! Be happy about it! Be very glad! For a tremendous reward awaits you up in heaven" (Matthew 5:11-12 TLB). And who knows? Because of the power of your story you may meet someone in heaven who is there because of your written or spoken words.

A Nonfiction Proposal to Grab a Book Editor's Attention

17

by Susan Titus Osborn

If you concentrate on the depth of your writing, God will take care of the breadth.

—Lee Roddy

Writing a nonfiction book is like eating an elephant. A person does not dare to attempt the project in one sitting!

Book Writing Process

1. Theme and Outline

Before you begin, decide what your main purpose is in writing this particular book. Where are you going? State your theme in one word. State it in one sentence. Know what you want to say, and say it. Keep to one subject.

Then create a preliminary outline before you begin the actual writing. This may change as the writing progresses, but you need something to start with. Your outline should be built around your chapter titles. Perhaps you have ten, twelve, or more.

Then write a paragraph about each chapter. Be aware that this may change drastically, but it is important to get down as much information as you can to use as a backbone for your book.

Each point must support the main theme. Each chapter, though self-contained, needs to promote the main idea. The major problem with most nonfiction book manuscripts that are rejected is they deviate from their premises. The writer tries to tell too many stories or attempts to make too many points in one book.

2. *First Rough Draft*

Find a large block of uninterrupted time and write all the information you can think of regarding the first chapter of your book. Don't get hung up in grammar, punctuation, or phraseology. Write whatever comes into your mind.

Writing the first rough draft is probably the most emotional birthing phase of the entire process. Once the words are on paper, you need to emotionally detach yourself from your "baby." Lay it aside for a week and emotionally remove yourself from it.

Begin another chapter or go on to another writing project. I suggest you go through this same writing process for each chapter of your book. Develop a focus and an outline before writing the first rough draft. It might be a good idea to write the easiest chapters first if you can determine those you can write quickly. Some of your chapters will be briefly outlined on your first rough drafts, while others may be in great detail.

3. *Self-editing*

Allow each chapter some time before beginning to self-edit. For example: If you have just written Chapter 3, you might go back to Chapter 1 and begin editing. Then look at the opening sentence and paragraph. Does it have a hook? Does it make the reader want to keep reading? Beginnings, for me, are the most difficult part of a manuscript to write. Often, I end up throwing out the first few paragraphs or the first page. I've found this a common problem on the manuscripts that come through our critique service.

Not only do I have trouble writing first paragraphs but also first chapters. I probably have one hundred hours in the first two chapters of my first nonfiction book, *You Start with One* (Thomas Nelson). Be careful not to get bogged down editing your first chapter. Move on and write a rough draft of the rest of the book before doing the final revision on the first chapter.

Go through each book chapter carefully. Look for spelling errors, missing punctuation, and incorrect use of grammar. Tighten your writing. Pull out unnecessary words and paragraphs. Keep your sentences short, but vary the length for interest. A sentence should seldom be over twenty-four words long. Gary Wall, vice president of Pioneer Clubs, says,"Learn to use words as if you had to pay $1.00 for each one."

The introduction to *The Elements of Style,* by William Strunk and E.B. White, says:"Vigorous writing is concise. A sentence should contain no unnecessary words, a paragraph no unnecessary sentences, for the same reason that a drawing should have no unnecessary lines and a machine no unnecessary parts."

Rearrange paragraphs and sentences to make the words flow better. Check your transitions to see if the paragraphs move smoothly one to another.

Are you meeting the reader's felt need as well as his real need in your message? Are you going to motivate the reader to change his life, to become a better person, or to move closer to Christ? This is the bottom line.

Book Proposal

Most publishing houses want to receive a book proposal rather than an entire manuscript. A few publishers prefer only a query letter. An editor spends an average of twenty minutes reviewing your book proposal, so it is imperative that you provide the correct material and that your manuscript looks professional. To determine the submission format for each publishing house, check Sally Stuart's *Christian Writers' Market Guide* to find the publisher's Web site, or send directly to the publisher for the writers' guidelines.

A book proposal is comprised of three parts:

- A cover letter
- A detailed chapter outline or a synopsis
- Three sample chapters

The cover letter should basically answer four questions:

1. Why are you qualified to write this book?
2. What is it about (told in one paragraph)?
3. Who is your audience?
4. Why will this book be marketable?

Also, make sure the publisher realizes you are familiar with his house and see that your book will fit into one of his book lines. This letter should be only one typewritten page if possible. The problem with most cover letters (and with most book proposals in general) is that they are too long and cumbersome. You may wish to include your résumé and a market analysis sheet, comparing your book to other similar books currently on the market. Tell the advantages of your book and why it will sell.

The chapter outline should be brief. Write a short paragraph summarizing each chapter to give the editor an overview of your book. This can be a vital tool for understanding the entire manuscript if the book proposal reaches the stage where it is considered by a publishing house committee.

Some publishing houses prefer a running synopsis of the book rather than a chapter outline, particularly for novels, but we are dealing basically with nonfiction book proposals in this chapter. See Chapter 8 for writing novels.

Three sample chapters are normally included in a book proposal. These should reflect the quality and substance of your book. Most editors prefer to receive the first three chapters. Some authors, however, prefer to send the first, middle, and last chapters; others prefer to include a chapter with specific significance. You be the judge regarding which is best for your manuscript, but you lose a sense of continuity if you don't send the first three chapters.

Be Informed

Read all the books and magazines you can. Try to spend as many hours reading as you do writing.

1. Pick up all the available freebies at writers' conferences. Become familiar with publishing houses and their book lines. You need to be

Sample Query (or Cover) Letter for a Book

Susie Writer
1 Longhand Land
Beach City, CA 90000
310-555-1212

July 2, 2001

Mr. Slickcover
Acquisitions Editor
Slickcover Book Company
1000 Everprint Street
Anytown, IL 60000

Dear Mr. Slickcover:

In reading your catalog, I see that you have a line of Sweet Story Books. I am in the process of writing a book of stories that I feel would fit your guidelines. In July, I attended the Christian Writers Conference at XYZ College where I met your acquisitions editor, Jerry Joyful. He suggested that I query you with my idea for a devotional book for newlyweds.

My education includes a BA in Religious Studies and an MA in Communications. I have been happily married for ten years, and my husband would provide input from the husband's viewpoint for the appropriate stories.

The book would provide fifty-two captivating and sometimes humorous stories for newlyweds. These will be taken from interviews and from my own experiences. The stories would provide examples of couples who have strong marriages and the obstacles they have overcome to keep them that way. It would provide a vehicle for newlyweds to open the door for better communication and deeper intimacy.

Let me know if you would be willing to see my book proposal for *Keeping the Home Fires Burning,* on speculation. I look forward to your response.

Yours in Him,
Susie Writer

comfortable with their styles and basic views before you write for them. Don't just read book catalogs, study them.

2. Decide which publishing houses you would like to write for. Go online and check out their Web sites. These can be found in Sally Stuart's *Christian Writers' Market Guide.* If you can't gain enough information from a publishing house's Web site, send a postcard. Ask for a sample copy of the latest catalog and the writers' guidelines. When you receive these, place them in folders in your file cabinet for easy access. Also, visit your local Christian bookstore. Talk to the owner, book buyer, or manager regarding similar books to the one you are writing.

3. Subscribe to *The Christian Communicator* and *The Advanced Christian Writer,* as well as other writing magazines such as *The Writer* and *Writer's Digest.* Purchase books on writing such as my book, *Just Write!,* and *A Complete Guide to Writing for Publication* available from me or from ACW Press. Also Writers Digest Books has a complete line of writing books.

Submission Format

Each publishing house receives thousands of book proposals annually, so yours must stand out to get attention. Be sure to use the correct submission format and address your envelope to a specific editor at the publishing house of your choice.

To give yourself an edge, attend a writers' conference and meet personally with a book acquisitions editor to establish a working relationship with him. Then, when it's time to mail your proposal, if he has asked you to send it in, you can write "Requested Material" on the envelope, and it will immediately reach that editor's desk. When he opens it, he can say, "I met her in person last summer and discovered her exciting idea for a potential book."

Sample First Page for Book Manuscript

The heading for the title page or first page of your book is important. There are several methods suggested in writing books and by authors. The next page shows a sample first page that I consider balanced and eye pleasing. For most book proposals, submit a title page and start your text on page two.

Sample First Page for a Book Manuscript

Susan Titus Osborn	Book Rights
3133 Puente Street	About 42,000 Words
Fullerton, CA 92635	© 2000 Susan Osborn
714-990-1532	Gift Book
Susanosb@aol.com	

Rest Stops for Single Moms

By Susan Titus Osborn

and Lucille Moses

Explanation of Headings

Left Heading

Always put your name, address, telephone number, and email address on the top left corner of the first page of the book proposal. If an editor needs to contact you, he has your information at his fingertips.

Right Heading

To maintain balance, these are the four items that go in the top right corner of the first page.

1. Rights

On the first line, list which rights you are offering. Normally if this is a book proposal, you are selling "Book Rights" for your manuscript.

The publishing house possesses *all* book publishing rights as long as your book stays in print. They usually have control of paperback rights on hardcover books and all subsidiary rights. These items are spelled out in detail in each individual contract. Do not sell chapters from your book without your publisher's permission.

Make sure your original contract calls for the copyright to be placed in your name. If this is done, once your book is out of print, the rights automatically revert to you in six months.

2. Word Count

On the second line, write the approximate number of words, rounded off to the nearest 100 words. Normally you can figure ten words to a line, 250 words to a page. Four pages are about 1,000 words.

3. Copyright

The third line is for your copyright information. If you are using Microsoft Word, click on "insert," then "symbols," and locate the symbol for copyright. This symbol is followed by the year and your legal name. Regarding books, the publisher will register your copyright with the Copyright Office of the Library of Congress in Washington, D.C.; remember, make sure this is registered in *your* name. If you are self-publishing a book, you can register your copyright with the Copyright Office for a nominal fee (see Chapter 12).

4. Miscellaneous

If this is a special type of book, is a series of books, or fits in a certain publishing line, put this information on the fourth line.

Subsequent Pages

Use a header with your last name, a key word from the title, and the chapter number in the top left hand corner of the second and all of the following pages. Put the page number in the top right corner of all but the first page. Number the entire book manuscript consecutively. For example:

Osborn-Chapter 4 Page 59

Finishing Touches

Once you have finished your book proposal, if you would like to have your manuscript professionally critiqued to make it more polished before sending it to a publisher, contact the Christian Communicator Manuscript Critique Service (see Appendix).

Here are some general principles to keep in mind.

1. Your manuscript should be double-spaced on white sixteen to twenty lb. paper with 1- to 1-1/2-inch margins all around. It is permissible to use computer or photocopying paper, but send a *clean* copy. Use 12 point type, Courier or Courier New font is best, but Times New Roman is acceptable. Leave the right margin unjustified (ragged). Double space your manuscript. Usually the preset standard margins on a computer are acceptable

2. The length of your book is determined by the publishing house you are writing for. Obtain the guidelines for each publisher you wish to submit your proposal to and adhere to those guidelines. If you submit a book proposal to only one publishing house at a time, it will get a closer look. If you submit to more than one house at a time, you *must* state that in your cover letter.

3. Make a second copy of your book proposal. Never mail your only copy, and never fold a manuscript. Place your manuscript in a 9x12 manila envelope or a Priority Mail envelope. Always include a self-addressed, stamped envelope (SASE). A Number 10 envelope is fine if you don't want the manuscript back, or you can just include your

email address instead for the editor's reply. Before you mail your manuscript, make a list of all the publishing houses that might consider buying it. If it comes back in the mail, then send it immediately to the next publishing house on your list.

4. Mail your manuscript to a specific editor. As was mentioned before, if you've met an editor at a conference, mail it to him. Never send it addressed to just the publishing house, or your manuscript may spend a considerable time in the unsolicited manuscript pile, known affectionately as the "slush pile." If an editor is interested in your proposal, it may take months for a decision to be made and a contract to be issued.

Contracts can take many different forms and can vary a great deal. The most common contract for a book is a royalty contract. Your typical book contract will be eight to fourteen pages in length. Be careful when signing a contract. Learn how to plow through the legal mumbo-jumbo to find the items you are really interested in. Lee Roddy covers this in Chapter 18.

Along with your contract comes a deadline. Be sure to pace yourself so you can meet that date. Don't *ever* miss a publisher's deadline! When your contract is issued, advertisement is placed in the publisher's catalog and press time is reserved. If you miss your deadline, the entire publishing process will be disrupted.

Once your book comes out in print, you are the best person to promote your own book. Plan to participate in autograph parties and to do radio call-in shows. For more information on tips for public speaking, see Chapters 20 and 21.

If you take the book-writing process in bite-sized chunks, chapter-by-chapter, you'll finish eating your elephant sooner than you anticipated. Plus, you won't develop indigestion. In fact, you'll whet your appetite for a new safari and will soon find yourself ready to start writing your next book. Your second book will take less time because of all you have learned writing the first one.

Books are lasting. They are here long after you are gone. They are accessible and available when the reader wants to read. Plus, they can go places where you cannot go. Never underestimate the power of your words, and may God richly bless your efforts.

Book Contracts, IRS 1099 Forms, Royalty Statements, and Agents

18

by Lee Roddy

Someday I hope to write a book where the royalties will pay for the copies I give away.

—Clarence Darrow

The serious author who is a Christian needs to deal with book contracts, questions regarding IRS 1099 forms, and royalty statements as well as writing a manuscript. In this chapter, I will explain some things you should watch for as well as help you to determine whether you could benefit from an agent or not at this time. I hope you will find this information valuable in dealing with publishers and agents. The author and publisher relationship should be a kind of partnership with a win-win objective for both, or equality, as Paul the Apostle taught.

Contracts

Most publishing contracts are much the same, with somewhere around fifty fairly standard clauses. Yet, many authors are woefully lacking in knowledge about the danger in some of those clauses. The result is that they get hurt, as I did. Hopefully, you can avoid that.

Two Principles

Let me suggest two principles needed to understand and negotiate book contracts. Then we'll examine a few clauses that I recommend against signing. There are also some other poor clauses that authors should know about.

- *Principle #1:* All contracts favor the publisher. If you don't believe that, try to get one to let you draw up the contract. I tried.
- *Principle #2:* All contracts are negotiable, so even a first-time author should always negotiate *some* changes in every contract. Successful negotiation comes from knowledge and a certain amount risk taking.

Negotiation Guidelines

Never sign the first contract offered unless you're desperate. Negotiate some improvements for yourself. To do that intelligently, you must obtain a copy of the proposed contract without indicating you'll accept it as is. You need to *see* what's actually being offered, because telephone discussions rarely give the full picture.

Even if you've signed previous contracts with a publisher, always carefully read *every* word of any new contract. They're sometimes changed without any indication to you that this is being done.

Determine who will do the negotiating for the publisher. If you're dealing with the business manager or other executive (not the editor) that means you're up against a professional while you're a babe in the woods.

As a professional author, don't start work until you've received a signed contract and advance. I've heard about some Christian authors who completed a book without a contract, only to have the publisher reject the work and pay nothing.

Deal Breakers

Watch out for the "deal breakers." Those are clauses that should make you consider passing up that publisher for a contract with more equitable terms. I recommend against such deal breakers as these:

Secrets

Perhaps the most odious clause that's come to my attention is one that forbids the author to show or discuss the contract with anyone except the publisher's representative. Most of us won't reveal our personal deals, but we should never be prohibited from discussing them if we want to do so.

Copyright

If you don't keep the copyright in your name, and the publisher sells the book or line of books to another house (that does happen), you'll receive no more royalties. That's because you don't have a contract with the other house.

I also strongly recommend not dealing with a publisher who claims that it's company policy for the copyright to be in the house's name. If you originated and wrote the book (not work-for-hire), keep the copyright.

To do that, make certain the agreement is specific, as: "The Publisher shall register the copyright of the work and all renewals of such copyright *in the name of the author* (strike out 'publisher' if it appears in the contract) in any and all countries of the world."

Net

Try substituting the word "wholesale" for "net" royalties, and it may help you to understand what a difference it makes to the author. I want a percentage of the book's cover price. That's a firm amount.

Some publishers argue that net comes out the same for the author in the long run. An answer might be, "If that's so, then you should have no objection to my wanting a percentage of the cover price instead of net."

Long ago, I took a proposed net contract to my accountant. He calculated that I would have to receive slightly more than double the offered net to equal a standard percentage of the cover price.

I've had authors tell me that some publishers claim they only do net, and some have even declared, "The whole industry does it." I disagree. The whole industry is not doing it.

Advances

Always get an advance against royalties (even on your first book, as I did), and make sure the contract says you don't have to give the money back unless you fail to deliver a manuscript. The publisher should have a strong interest in recovering that investment. As your works sell, advances will be larger.

Option

If you sign this clause, it means you can't sell your next book to any other house until the publisher with whom you've signed decides whether to accept or reject it. That's called the right of first refusal.

Strike the option clause because it is grossly unfair to the author. Example: The publisher often doesn't have to consider your next book for a year or two, and then has an inordinate amount of time to decide about accepting or rejecting it. The only option I sign is one that gives the publisher first choice on the next book for the same characters in a series.

If you sold one novel, you can sell another—perhaps to another house and on better terms.

Cross-Collateralized

This means that if you have two or more books with a publishing house, and one makes money but the other doesn't, you won't earn any royalties. Years ago, I had the experience of having a publisher cancel a line after I'd written two novels. My first novel repaid its advance and should have earned money thereafter, but the second book never had a chance to repay its advance because the line was discontinued. The "tie across" clause kept me from ever receiving any royalties at all.

That dangerous clause reads something likes this: "Publisher agrees to pay author a total advance (recoupable from future royalties and over all works and subsidiary sales covered by this agreement), etc."

Here's a better alternative: "Each book shall be considered separately for royalty and royalty advance purposes (i.e., no monies due from the author on one book shall be deducted from the royalties for another book)." Or: "For royalty accounting purposes, each book by the author shall be counted as separate from any other book."

Non-Compete Clause

This once appeared in my new contract. As I read it, the publisher wanted me to agree that I would not write anything that the house might consider competitive to the novels I was going to write for that publisher. I refused to sign it, fearful that this might be interpreted to mean that I couldn't write any more juvenile novels for another publisher.

Unspecified Rights

This is particularly important in today's exploding technology. Bargain to keep as many rights as possible, and don't sign away any rights not clearly specified in the contract, such as games, interactive software, video, audio tapes, books on tape, etc. Beware of words like display rights, electronic publishing rights, storage, retrieval, etc.

The contract would better read like this: "All rights now known or to be known throughout the universe that are not specifically granted herein shall be reserved to the Author for the Author's sole use and disposition."

Subsidiary Rights

When I started writing professionally, I never expected lightning to strike at all, let alone repeatedly. Who would have guessed that six books I wrote would also be produced as movies, a TV series, video, etc.? I later learned about ancillary rights, so now I suggest keeping as many rights as possible.

Try to make some other rights conditional. For example, my books are sold in many foreign countries. I learned that it's possible to negotiate the contract so that if the publisher doesn't sell the overseas rights within a reasonable time (like eighteen months) after publication, all such rights promptly and automatically revert to me.

Held Against Returns

Publishers often hold back a percentage of the author's royalties as protection against books that are returned from bookstores. By reading trade journals and talking to other knowledgeable people, I found that 8 to 10 percent is reasonable to be held against returns on heavily promoted Christian frontlist titles. This knowledge came in handy when a publisher's contract called for 20 percent. It was negotiated down to a fair figure. I've received a deal where withholding was only 2 percent, and another where none was withheld. These are logically based on the sales track record.

If unfair or dangerous clauses are to ever be eliminated from contracts, authors must become more knowledgeable. Perhaps these tips will help you avoid pitfalls when negotiating your next book contract.

IRS Form 1099-Misc

One of the newest issues to face the professional author is the way Christian publishers issue IRS Form 1099-Misc (ten-ninety-nine). The traditional author's contract with the publisher (where an agent is involved) specifies that the house will give the author a specific dollar amount as an advance against royalties, and that a certain percentage of the author's royalties will go to the agent.

The recent entry of literary agents into the Christian publishing field has resulted in some houses taking a unique approach, both in paying royalties and in reporting the author's and agent's earnings to the IRS. That's where I am uneasy.

I have discussed this concern with the Authors Guild of America, three Christian houses that practice this system, and a couple of agents. None of the answers I've received have put my mind at rest.

Traditionally, trade (secular) publishers send an author's advance and royalty checks to the agent representing the author. The agent deducts his 15 percent and sends the balance to the author.

However, Christian publishers are sending the author's 85 percent directly to him and the remaining 15 percent to the agent. This practice avoids the traditional system where agents sometimes hold an author's earnings for an unfair amount of time. I like the Christian house system, except for the tax reporting part.

Annually, the Christian house sends its IRS 1099 to the author so he can file his income tax. However, this form shows only the net paid to the author, instead of the gross, minus the commission. I'd like to see both figures given, for good reason.

What happens when an author files his income taxes showing the gross he earned from the publisher (by contract), but the 1099 form shows a lesser amount? Couldn't there be complications that may not surface to bite until a few years later?

I'm afraid that the publisher's 1099 figures are misleading because they officially show the author's income is 15 percent less than he actually grossed. But more importantly, it seems to me that there's a possibility the government may challenge the author's right to deduct the agent's 15 percent as a legitimate business expense.

According to the contract, the author was paid a gross figure. Of that gross, the author paid the agent his 15 percent. That's an author's deductible business expense. But the author's contract with the publisher is not a part of the government's 1099. Only the net paid the author is given; there's no mention of the gross.

It seems to me that, under the present system, the IRS could claim the publisher paid the agent, not the author. The government therefore might challenge the author's deduction of the commission.

I have been assured there's not going to be a problem, but the only assurance that counts is from the IRS. No author I know has time to hassle with them or lose valuable writing time if the issue comes up.

Royalty Statements

I don't think I've ever met a writer who was completely satisfied with his publisher's royalty statements. Neither have I known an author who could properly read and understand most such documents.

Any changes in this field must naturally come from the publishing houses, but I doubt they'll do that unless they know other publishing houses are sending better statements to authors.

However, I'm happy to say that at least one publisher has made major strides in providing a readable and comprehensive statement. Another house recently improved its reports. Others could take a lesson from those publishers who are making progress in this area.

Guidelines

Let's consider some guidelines that should logically be in every author's royalty statement beyond the usual (name, social security number, etc.)

I like all data about each book listed on one page, not several. One page for each title can show everything I've ever wanted to know, from the obvious (quarter reported, earnings, books sold and in print, etc.) to other pertinent information that should be available to the author.

Some authors may be content to simply know how much they made the last quarter or the past six months and how much the work has earned life to date. However, I believe that a good steward should also look beyond the obvious monetary consideration to the ministry aspects. Ministry is the reason most of us write in this field, but the Scriptures teach that a workman is worthy of his hire. The more units sold, the greater the ministry possibilities.

In fact, I don't know of any house that keeps a book in print unless it's paying its own way. That means the book must earn more for the publisher than its cost to keep it in circulation. The house will be out of ministry if good business practices are ignored. Royalty statements show a book's profitability or liability, and the author needs to carefully study those statements.

Clarifying

Let's explore what the royalty statement should show about income. You not only need to know how much you were paid this quarter per book, but if the amount is net or gross. Two nets may be involved in figuring this part.

If an agent is used, the royalty statement should include both the gross and the net earned by each book title. That's because you paid the agent 15 percent more than your statement shows you earned—if it's only listing the net you received.

The other net figure revolves around units sold this quarter at full price and how many were sold at various discounts. That includes book clubs, special editions, foreign sales, book sets, etc.

You need to know total units sold this quarter and total units life to date, plus dollars earned this quarter and dollars earned life to date. Then you can figure out how much you actually earned on each book this quarter, as well as the amount earned since it was published. This figure may seem lower than you thought.

Right Perspective

High volume sales mean greater ministry opportunities, plus more for the publisher and the author. Remember, in today's real world, your home, church, etc., cannot effectively minister without money. The royalty statement is an accurate report card on your efforts, but should be kept in perspective.

Unfortunately, the royalty statement cannot directly show ministry effectiveness, but the monetary figures give some indication of its possibilities. Unsold books can't minister; royalty statements show what is ministering.

Now let's look at the numbers. It is important to know the total books in print for each title, for each series, and for all your books. I tried keeping my own figures, but with fifty-one novels now in print, I miscalculated and came up short of what one publisher's royalty statement showed. In that series, I had passed half a million copies without knowing it. The proper royalty statement showed my error, so I updated my calculations.

Reprints

A problem can arise when the author isn't notified that a book has gone back to print. This would not happen if the statement carried the date of first publication, plus the number of each title reprinted that quarter. This would allow the author to calculate which books consistently sell well and which don't. He can also try to figure out why and avoid those kinds of faults in future writings.

I think it's rare for a publisher to list reprint dates and press runs, but it's an area for publishers to consider in updating their forms.

The above should be sufficient to help you better understand your royalty statement. Hopefully, it may lead you to politely suggest to some publishers what an author would like to see improved in reporting systems. After all, writing and publishing is a partnership where each party should get what he deserves.

Agents

A selling author with several titles on the market wrote me with a common question: Should I obtain a literary agent?

I sold fifty-some books without an agent, and about a dozen since then. I've also talked to many selling authors, some who favor agents, and others who don't. These combined experiences may help you in considering whether it's time to have someone represent you, and how to judge which is the right agent. Let's start by asking pertinent questions.

Definition

What is meant by a "literary agent"? A literary agent is one who sells an author's works to publishers for a percentage of the initial gross sale, plus a commission on all subsequent sales of the book or ancillary rights.

There apparently are no laws governing who can call himself a literary agent. Example: Some "agents" charge a reading fee and otherwise make money directly off their clients, instead of indirectly by selling the authors' works.

Until recently, there were two professional literary organizations. One was for "agents" who charged a reading fee. The other group limited membership to agents who only received a percentage of what they sold. Then both groups merged, blurring the distinction on agents.

To me, a literary agent is one who gets a percentage of what he sells for an author. No sale, no money.

Motives

Why do you want a literary agent? Some authors are poor business people. However, learning to sell your own work is part of writing, especially until you establish a track record. When you're selling regularly, it may be time to consider an agent.

I signed with one when my workload was so heavy there wasn't time to properly negotiate with publishers. It's practical to let a qualified representative handle business deals, leaving the author more free time to write.

Why should an agent represent you? A good agent is a sales person who gets 15 percent of what he sells. If he can't make money off of your writing, there's no reason for him to represent you. So before you approach an agent, be ready to show what's in it for him.

Qualifications

What should I look for in an agent? The first thing is experience as an editor or publisher, plus demonstrated selling skills. His job is selling, but he must have inside knowledge of the field.

An agent is going to evaluate you on the salability of your product and on your production capability. You must pre-judge the agent on his qualifications. Be bold. Ask:

- For whom did he work as an editor or publisher? When? How long? Whom does the agent know inside various publishing houses where you hope to sell?

- Who are the agent's clients? Do you recognize any of the authors' names? Are they all straight percentage clients? How many books has the agent sold? Titles? Sales history?
- Does the agent charge for telephone calls, printing, etc.? That should be part of his/her cost of doing business and covered by the agent's 15 percent.

Contracts

Ask to see the agent's contract before agreeing to be represented. Be sure everything is clearly spelled out. Determine whether the agent's heirs continue to receive 15 percent of all previous sales, even if the heirs no longer do anything for you.

If you sell the work yourself, does the agent still get a percentage? Remember, that's fifteen cents out of every dollar your book makes while it's in print, plus ancillary rights over the years. Fifteen pennies may not sound like much, but if you gross $100,000 annually, that's $15,000, or $150,000 commission in ten years.

Communication

An often-overlooked element is the importance of regular communication. In addition to keeping the agent informed of what you're doing, you need some kind of regular report from him. He may balk, citing various excuses, but on-going communication is essential. You should know (preferably monthly) to whom your work has been submitted, what the editor's response was, etc.

This information will be invaluable if you ever change agents so that the new one doesn't submit material already rejected by an editor, etc.

As a Christian who is an author, you need an agent who clearly understands your faith and preferably is also a believer who can represent you before Christian publishers and crossover trade editors.

Make sure your agent's contract has a "divorce" clause, as allowing sixty days written notice by either party to end the relationship.

Search

Where do I find a good agent? Some are listed in writers' publications such as *The Christian Communicator,* in books such as the *Christian*

Writers' Market Guide, or with the Authors Guild. I think it's critical to talk to many agents. I met dozens at secular writers' meetings, but none at Christian conferences. I've also met some at conventions for the Christian Booksellers Association. Or an agent may call you, as happened to me.

I trust that this information is helpful although it is certainly not complete. I hope it will be useful in negotiating your next contract, dealing with publishers, and deciding whether on not to use an agent.

The Marketing Game 19

by Sally E. Stuart

After being turned down by numerous publishers, he had decided to write for posterity.

—George Ade

At the end of a session I once taught on marketing, a lady rushed up to me visibly excited. "I can't believe this," she said, fairly bubbling over. "I work in marketing all the time, but it never occurred to me that marketing my writing would be just like marketing any other product."

I nodded in agreement, but she went on before I could respond. "I can use all the marketing techniques I already know. I don't know why that never occurred to me."

I don't know either. If there is one thing writers should understand before reading this chapter, or trying to market their work, it is that any marketing principles they know will apply to manuscript submissions. Keep that in mind as you learn how to sell what you write.

Where to Start

One of the primary mistakes most writers make—whether beginners or more advanced—is that they write an article or book before looking for a publisher. That is one reason so many manuscripts go unsold. If you don't start with a target in mind, it's no wonder you never hit anything. It is important to look at marketing as part of the writing process, not as a separate step that is taken at the end of the creative phase.

Even before you start writing, there is some preliminary work that will make your job easier. First, decide what kinds of writing you are most interested in. It might be teen short stories, adult Bible studies, feature articles, or how-to pieces.

You will likely be interested in more than one area, so make a list of all the types of writing that interest you. This list is meant to be a worksheet, so write them down even if you're not positive you will pursue those areas. You can always cross items out later.

Next, think specifically about the people you will write for. What age or interest groups are you most qualified for or most interested in writing for? Children? Teens? Singles? Young Marrieds? Senior Adults? Parents? Men? You decide, and make a list of possibilities. These are your potential "target audiences."

Now, it's time to think about possible topics. Some of you are writing because you have a specific story that must be told; because you are a pastor with insights to share; because you feel strongly about a subject such as marriage, family, abortion, or home schooling; or because you want to share your expertise in some area. Make a list of topics you are interested in or feel qualified to write about.

Three lists (types of writing, potential audience, and topics) will be the basis for your preliminary market work. Your job is to pick out three or four primary areas and start determining what the best markets will be for those areas. For example, you might decide to aggressively market traditional poetry, feature articles on education concerns, and self-help articles on marriage. Before you actually start writing, you will want to find out who might buy these particular topics or types of writing.

Using the Market Guide

Your primary resource for this next step is an appropriate market guide. If you want to publish in the Christian market, that would be the current edition of the *Christian Writers' Market Guide*. If your interest is in secular areas, it might be *Writer's Market*, or any number of special guides available for specialty areas such as novels, children's markets, ethnic markets, etc. For our purposes, we'll refer to the *Christian Writers' Market Guide*.

With any market guide, it is important to spend some time getting acquainted with the content, set-up, and how-to-use-this-book information. Since this is your primary tool, you must feel comfortable with it and practice its regular use. Once you understand how to use it, look up your primary interests in the topical listings.

For example, let's start with marriage. Under marriage in the topical listings, you will find a list of periodicals interested in that topic. Keep in mind that even though a periodical is listed in that section, it may not necessarily be a good potential market for your articles on marriage. You must spend some time becoming acquainted with each of those periodicals and decide which ones offer the best potential for your material.

You may cross some periodicals off the list because they are connected with a denomination you're not in theological agreement with or because they have a stance on marriage you don't share. Some may not pay (or pay enough), some may want all rights (and you want to sell only first or one-time rights), some may pay on publication (and you want to be paid on acceptance), some may not be copyrighted, or some may use very little freelance material. For these and various other reasons you may decide to cross off some of those markets.

After you have eliminated those you aren't interested in, start looking more closely at those that do interest you. Carefully read each individual listing and look for markets that appeal to you. Periodicals are like people. Each has its own personality, likes, and dislikes. Just as you select friends based on mutual interest and concern, you will also find periodicals that will become "friends," based on the same kind of compatible qualities.

In the primary listings, you will find information on how to order sample copies and writers' guidelines for each periodical you want to know more about. Send for those and spend some time reading the guidelines and copies cover-to-cover. Many publishers now make their guidelines available on their Web site, or they can be requested by email. That will save a lot of time and postage. If a publisher has a Web site (that information will be listed in the market guide), be sure to spend some time studying the site to learn as much as possible about the publisher and its unique focus. As you study each market, you will likely discard some you don't care for and select those you want to pursue.

Study the select periodicals more closely by doing an analysis of each one, noting such things as: length of articles, paragraphs, titles, and sentences; types of articles used; slant; unique terms; etc. By the time you finish this, you should have a clear idea of which periodicals you want to write for.

Under "Marriage" on a marketing sheet, list these periodicals. Repeat the same process for each of those major areas you have decided to target. You can take this process a step further by asking each of these periodicals to send you a copy of its most recent demographic study, which will give you more specific information about its target audience.

It's a good idea to compile a notebook of your writers' guidelines and any analysis notes you come up with in the above study. Use alphabetical dividers and put them in alphabetically by title of the periodical (or book publisher). Keep this on or near your desk for easy access. Sample copies can also be kept alphabetically in a box or magazine holder by category—e.g., one for marriage, one for poetry, or whatever your primary topics are. Keep them handy for quick reference until you become more familiar with them.

Getting Ready to Write

There are some important steps to consider each time you approach a new writing project. Answer or follow through on the following steps:

- State in one sentence the primary focus and goal of this piece of writing.
- Who wants or needs to hear this message? Who is your audience? Define the group by age, denomination, interest, etc.

- Decide what format is best for conveying this message to this audience. Should it be a feature article, a how-to article, a short story, or a Bible study? Or, could it be adapted to more than one format to reach different audiences?
- After making the above decisions, start a list of potential markets based on the analysis of markets you did earlier. Choose the market you want to try first and check to see how long your piece should be, whether you need to send a query, etc. Fill out a form or sheet with this pertinent information and keep it in a file or notebook next to your computer so you will know how to proceed when you are ready to start writing.

Now you will be ready to write a piece that will have one or several potential markets, based on specific market research, not on a wild (and usually incorrect) guess. Granted, this is not an overnight process, but any time you spend studying the markets is going to save you time and money that would be lost in writing articles that no one wants to buy. It also prevents you from wasting postage by sending manuscripts to the wrong publishers.

The greatest investment in time comes with the initial analysis. The more time you spend with these publications, the better acquainted you will become with them and the less time you will have to spend marketing each piece. Eventually you will know these new "friends" well enough that you won't have to renew your acquaintance each time you need a market.

Query Letters

As the market guide indicates, a good number of periodicals require that you send a query letter instead of a complete manuscript. A query is simply a sales letter in which you try to sell the editor on your idea. It's a job application and sample of your writing rolled into one. It needs to indicate why this publisher is the one to publish your manuscript and why you are the one to write it.

The market analysis you have already done will give you the resources you need to convince the editor that you know a lot about his publication and audience, and that you can write to meet his specific needs. Be sure to reflect that information in your query. For example,

"Since 60 percent of your target audience is young marrieds, this article will provide much needed help for those early adjustment years."

Keep your query as short as possible—one to one-and-a-half pages is best—while at the same time being as specific as possible. An editor must have enough information about what you are offering so he can make an informed decision as to whether or not he is interested in seeing it. Following is a list of things to include:

1. A grabber opening to catch the editor's attention. Your query opening can even be the lead to your article if it's particularly compelling.
2. Include examples of what will be in the article, such as a quotation from an authority, statistics, or a strong anecdote.
3. Give the editor a reason he should publish it.
4. Give your writing credentials, qualifications, special skills, and reason for writing this piece. Also, identify and clarify your viewpoint. If you don't have any writing credentials, don't say so.
5. Indicate a sharp focus. This isn't an article on marriage, but an article on how newly married couples deal with in-laws.
6. Give specifics as to length, availability of photos, and when you can have the manuscript ready.
7. Don't mention money unless you have written for this publication before and you need to ask them about covering travel or research expenses necessary to getting the story. They will determine what you will be paid for the piece based on their established payment scale.
8. Some of the things you will include are not as easily definable—such as emotion and enthusiasm for the topic or a sense of who you are as a person and a writer. Let your personality come through. You don't want to be too business-like or too folksy. Be yourself, but be professional. If you are offering a humorous piece, let your ability to write humor show in your query. If your topic is a highly emotional one, show your sensitivity and caring.
9. Conclude with a postscript in which you indicate your willingness to work with the editor in developing a manuscript that will best meet the needs of his readers.

Selling a Book Manuscript

Up to now we have talked primarily about how to sell to periodicals. Selling a book can involve many of the same steps, but it is unique in other ways. The process takes more time, but then most of us don't sell as many books in our lifetime as we do articles.

As with articles, you will begin by deciding which topics you could write a book on and who your audience might be. With books, this step is even more critical, and a step you won't want to rush. Work with your topic idea until you can write down the slant and purpose of the book in one specific, concrete sentence. If you cannot distill the idea into a sentence, you are not ready to write the book.

Once you can do that, you must be able to convince a publisher that there is a specific and easily definable market for your book. Think of it in terms of to whom the publisher will market it. If you were to walk into a bookstore and see a big display of your books inside the front door, what would be on the sign over the display? To whom would the bookstore be trying to pitch those books? The publisher expects this audience to be specific, but also broad enough that there are plenty of potential customers. For example, "all parents" is too broad, "parents of deaf children" is too narrow, but "parents of preschoolers" is probably right.

The process of studying potential markets is much the same as it was with periodicals. Look up the topic of your book in the topical book listings in the market guide and follow the same steps to determine the best markets for your particular idea. Study the guidelines, Web sites and catalogs. The catalogs will be especially helpful in determining which publishers are potential markets. Start with an overview of the whole catalog and ask if you would be comfortable having your book included with everything else they are offering.

Are you basically in agreement with a particular house's doctrinal stance and the types of books it publishes? If not, cross it off your list. If you like what you see, find the section where your book would be listed. Is there a large number of books in your general topic area (let's say marriage books)? If so, that house may be a good choice. If not, you might want to find one better known for that type of book.

If the catalog contains a lot of marriage books, is there one on the specific area yours will cover? If so, go elsewhere. A publisher will not usually publish a book that is in direct competition to another book in its line.

What you are looking for is a publisher that has a good line of marriage books, not one like yours. You want to feel confident your book would complement the line of marriage books the publisher already has.

After you have determined which might be potential publishers, go to a Christian bookstore for some additional marketing analysis. Find the section on marriage books and see what is there. Make some notes on the following questions:

- Which publishers have the most marriage books on the shelf?
- Which book covers are most attractive and catch your eye?
- Which books have the quality of covers, paper, illustrations, and type style you would want on your book?
- Are there any books on the shelf that cover the same content yours will? (If so, you may want to buy those and read them.)

While you're there, talk to the store's book buyer (if it's a large store, you might be wise to call ahead and make an appointment). Tell the buyer about your idea and ask things like:

- Is there a demand for or an interest in this type book?
- What are the most popular books on this topic?
- Which publisher is best known for this type of book?

As writers, we are usually so interested in selling our book to someone—anyone—that we don't think enough about what happens to our book after it is published. Unless the bookstores buy it, it is not going to sell. Therefore, it is important for you to know which publisher a bookstore (or distributor) is likely to frequent to buy a particular type of book.

For example, you may sell your novel to a publisher, but unless that publisher already has a significant line of novels to attract a bookstore, it won't sell many copies. A bookstore will go readily to a publisher who has a good, solid line of novels, but usually won't bother with one who has only two or three from which to choose. Put at the top of your list those publishers who have the most significant lines for your type of book.

At this point, I suggest you stop and take a close look at your book idea in light of the information you collected on the potential market and competition. Ask yourself honestly if there is a need and a market for this book. The truth is, unless you have something new or different to say on your topic, or you can say it better than the books already out there, there really isn't a need for your book.

If you aren't confident that you have a strong possibility of selling, or if you don't believe strongly enough in this project to see it through some potentially discouraging times ahead, now is the time to abandon this idea and move on to one that will stand these tests.

If you are still convinced you have a winning manuscript, evaluate your market study and bookstore information and select a first choice, but also make a list of other potential publishers you can go to if the first one rejects it. The market guide will tell you what those publishers want to see initially. Some will want only a query letter, some a complete manuscript, but most prefer a book proposal and sample chapters.

If you have never sold a book before, you will probably have to complete the book before a publisher will offer you a contract, but that doesn't mean you need to complete it before you contact a publisher. Generally, you will do enough research or preparation so you can know what will be included in the book, including the chapter breakdown, before you approach a publisher.

If the publisher asks for a query letter only, you must write a letter to sell him on your idea so he will ask to see your book proposal or entire manuscript. The query letter should again tell him specifically what you plan to accomplish, why you are the one to write it, and why you think this publisher is the one to publish it. Use some of the specific information you learned about this publishing house in your market research. If an editor is interested, he will either ask you to send the completed manuscript, or he will ask for a book proposal.

The Book Proposal

A book proposal has a specific purpose and a specific structure. With all the writers trying to woo editors to publish their books—and with so few being published each year—it is important that your proposal contains all the information a publisher needs. Also, it must be clean, crisp, and professional looking. If you have an older or dot matrix printer, it would be worthwhile to take a disk of your manuscript to a print shop where you could get laser copies made. It does make a marked difference in your presentation.

Following is a list of what needs to be included in your book proposal. Don't crowd it. Leave as much white space as you can so the proposal looks easy to read.

- Cover Letter: Keep it short—no more than one page. Simply introduce the subject and whet the editor's appetite to read your proposal. If you have someone who has agreed to write a foreword or introduction to your book, include that information here.
- Page 1: Include the following—
  - (a) Working title. (You can include a list of alternate titles if you're not sold on the one you picked.)
  - (b) Thesis statement. This is that theme statement you came up with before you started writing your book.
  - (c) Thesis paragraph. Expand the statement into a paragraph telling the points you will develop.
- Page 2 (or more if needed): Table of contents. Titles only. Not needed if you have no chapter titles.
- Next few pages: Chapter-by-chapter synopsis. Write a paragraph synopsis of each chapter telling specifically what will be covered in that chapter. An editor should be able to read through this and know exactly what the book is about and the primary points you will make. For example, don't say, "This chapter will include the ten best ways to communicate in your marriage." Instead, briefly list the ten ways. Leave about six lines between each synopsis or balance them on the pages, trying not to break a synopsis at the end of a page.
- Next Page: Define the potential market for your book, including competition. Tell who will buy the book, what other books there are on the market that are similar to yours (or might be competitive), and how your book differs from those.

- Next Page: Author's credentials. Include writing credits and any life experience that qualifies you to write this book.
- Next: Proposed format, including estimated number of pages, number of chapters, number of words; as well as any planned appendices, charts, photographs, or illustrations.
- Next: Delivery date. When you expect you can have the book completed. Be realistic. Always add two to four weeks to the delivery date you think you can meet.
- Next: Possibility of series, additions, leader's guide, audio, video, merchandising, etc. Share here any ideas you have for expanding the book into a series or other related products. This is your baby, so include all realistic ideas for expanding the concept of the book.
- Next Page: Author's preface. This can be included here since it provides a sample of your writing style and often includes your reasons for writing the book. This is especially helpful if the publisher wants only a proposal and no sample chapters.
- Last section: Sample chapters. The market guide will indicate how many. The general rule is to send the first chapter (so the editor can see how you approach the subject), the one you think is the best or that includes your strongest material, and the most "risky" one (the one the publisher is most likely to disagree with or have a problem with). Some publisher prefer the first three chapters (see market guide for preference). If the market guide states that the publisher wants more than three, simply send a good balance of content.

All this material can be sent loose in an envelope, or you can put it in a professional-looking folder of some kind. There is no set length for a book proposal, but the idea is to include all the information a publisher needs to make a decision without making it so long he will put off reading it. An editor should be able to read through it quickly and easily and have a clear idea of what you are proposing when he gets to the last page. If he has a lot of questions when he finishes, you probably have not done a good job on your proposal.

A clear, concise proposal will give the editor confidence in your ability to produce a publishable book. If your proposal is sloppy and poorly organized, the editor will likely reject your proposal unless you have such a compelling topic that he's willing to work harder than usual to produce a good book.

Summary

In all that you have learned about marketing, I hope one of the primary things is that marketing is not an afterthought. It is as much a part of the writing process as putting the words on paper. Marketing cannot be ignored. With the constantly increasing competition in the Christian market, the days are past when you can write an article or book about what's on your mind and then go looking for a place to sell it. If you don't know where you are going to send a piece before you write it, you aren't likely to ever sell it.

It takes a little more time up front to learn your markets. However, as soon as you learn those markets and put out some effort to keep up with new ones, marketing will cease to be a stumbling block to publication. Once you know the players, then learn the rules and play by them, you can't help but win the marketing game.

The Business Side of Speaking

20

by Kathy Collard Miller

We often get ahead of ourselves—wanting to be a big name speaker or author. Focus on the next step and you won't get distracted.

—Georgia Shaffer

Our goal and desire as speakers is to impart wisdom and understanding so that lives will be touched and changed. Yet, we can't do that without marketing ourselves and operating our ministry like a business. Some people may cringe at calling our speaking ministry a business, but God wants us to be good stewards. That is how we honor the Lord. Psalm 49:3 says, "My mouth will speak words of wisdom; the utterance from my heart will give understanding."

Promoting Yourself

In 1980, when I was writing a book about my experience as a former child abuser, I had no desire to be a public speaker. However, as I told a new church acquaintance about the topic of my book, she said, "You should share your story with our women's group!"

I replied, "No! I don't intend to tell anyone!" I was still so ashamed of what I'd done that I couldn't bear the thought. Somehow writing it for a book seemed distant from telling people in person. She persisted and mentioned she would tell the leader of our women's group about my story. Several weeks later, that woman asked me to speak. Although I felt inadequate, the Lord had begun to give me peace about it, and I said "yes."

With trepidation I prepared my speech, practiced it, and then presented it to several friends. I still felt inadequate.

On the morning of my speaking engagement, I arrived at church and learned that they expected over one hundred women to attend, far above their usual number. Now I was really nervous! Yet, I sensed the Lord strengthening me. As I gave my talk, I knew from the women's response that God was using my words. I was hooked!

Then, when women shared how meaningful my talk was, I was sure I wanted to do more public speaking. I hadn't expected such an emotional response within me or from the audience. God was gracious to use my feeble attempt to share His message.

Now that I've been speaking for over twenty years, I blush thinking of that first attempt. I basically read my written-out speech while trying to have as much eye contact as possible.

We all have to start somewhere though, and I was eager to continue this new adventure. Through word of mouth and the contacts made through my books, the invitations increased over the years.

You may be eager to speak and wonder how you can receive invitations. Here are some ideas:

- Tell everyone you know that God has called you to speak.
- Instead of mailing a Christmas card, write out a family newsletter and talk about your new calling. Mail it to as many people as possible.
- Contact your local Rotary Club, library, and Chamber of Commerce and volunteer your services as a speaker.
- Network with other speakers. Ask them to refer you when they receive invitations and can't fulfill them. Attend writers'

conferences and speakers' seminars where you'll learn and network with other speakers.

- Be willing to take low-paying and non-paying opportunities to test your material and make contact with people who may then be able to refer you to others.
- Have your talk taped so that you'll have tapes to send out to those who inquire.
- Send your Ministry Information Sheet (see next section) along with a tape to the churches in your area. Although this method of "cold calling" isn't usually highly effective, God can use it.

With all these efforts, cultivate an attitude of trusting God to put your name before meeting planners. Psalm 127:1 warns, "Unless the Lord builds the house, its builders labor in vain. Unless the Lord watches over the city, the watchman stands guard in vain." My paraphrase says, "Unless the Lord generates a speaking engagement, I market in vain. Unless God directs my ministry, my efforts will be pointless."

I have been amazed many times at how word about my ministry reaches meeting planners. God certainly accomplishes His purposes in creative ways. If God influences the hearts of kings (Proverbs 21:1), then He can certainly direct the hand of meeting planners.

Several years ago, I received a letter in the mail from someone who had heard me speak. I was amazed to discover it was a year old! I quickly telephoned the writer and explained that I had just received her letter. She replied, "Maybe this timing is even better. I'm on the committee for our women's retreat, and I'd love to recommend you for speaking."

She did, and I spoke for their area retreat several months later. God's timing had used a year-old letter!

When a meeting planner initially contacts you—hopefully not by a year-old letter—having a separate business telephone will present a professional atmosphere. Even though my office is in a bedroom of my home, I have a separate business line. When I answer it, "The Millers' office, Kathy speaking," I sound professional and give confidence to that meeting planner. Having a two-year-old or teenager answer might not be quite as impressive. Plus, you might not receive the message from a teenager.

Before I converted a spare bedroom into my office several years ago, my desk was initially in my bedroom. When I heard my business line ring and rushed from the kitchen where I'd been chopping vegetables, I had to inwardly giggle. As I answered, I glanced around and noticed my unmade bed and boxes of books stacked against the wall. Sometimes, the meeting planner paused in confusion and asked, "Is this Kathy Collard Miller? I thought I'd get a secretary." I was often tempted to reply, "Oh, she's off today," but instead I assured her she had reached the right person.

Ministry Information Sheet

One of the most useful tools you'll need for promoting yourself is your Ministry Information Sheet (MIS). Regardless of the style, color, or page format you use, here are the basics you'll need to include:

1. An opening paragraph (or two)

It should make the meeting planner think positively about you. My MIS begins: "If you want both power and practicality included in your program, then Kathy Collard Miller is the speaker for you! Kathy portrays God's healing power and communicates practical principles from His Word. Tall, slim, with flashing blue eyes, this pretty mother of two radiates warmth and compassion. With her quick smile, Kathy conveys the depth of her commitment to help others heal emotional hurts as well as to show them how to identify and eliminate destructive behavior."

Don't be shy about your positive qualities. If you feel awkward writing it, ask someone to help you.

2. Your story or background

What compelled you to become a speaker? If you have a dramatic story, tell it briefly. I mention in mine how God delivered me from being an abusive mother and how He healed my troubled marriage.

3. Speaking and writing credits

Mention whether you have written for magazines, newspapers, etc., or if you have authored books. Include any TV or radio programs where you've been interviewed. If you don't have these credits, omit this part. You can add them later as those opportunities arise.

4. List available topics

Don't worry if you haven't already written a talk. If a topic is of interest to you and you have some idea of what you might cover, write a paragraph about it. You can begin to develop it and have it ready when the time comes.

5. Events

Include what event(s) your talk could be most appropriate for and what length of time you could speak. Possible events might be: retreats, mother-daughter banquets/luncheons, marriage conferences, parenting groups, workshops, women's meetings, or family conferences.

Here's a sample description of one of my talks: "*Find Contentment in a Disappointing World.* Happiness is what happens to you, contentment is something you choose. Yet, contentment is a difficult goal to attain. Therefore, Kathy discusses contentment cheaters like our physical bodies, people, problems, and possessions, along with biblical principles for attaining and maintaining this worthy goal. Especially effective for full-day seminar or weekend retreat. Time: One to four hours."

6. A photo

Use the services of a professional photographer.

7. The "close"

Here's the wording on my information sheet: "Most of Kathy's presentations combine to fill a half or full-day seminar or weekend retreat. Kathy's ministry has touched audiences nationally and internationally, and she'll touch your audience as well with God's healing power and practical ideas for changing hearts and lives. Kathy has audiotapes available for preview. For more information, please contact: (my name, address, and telephone number, and email address)."

If the MIS you are preparing will be used by an agent, then list the agent's name, address, and telephone number.

Having your MIS available will present you as a professional as well as give you confidence.

Contact Sheet

When your business line rings and a meeting planner inquires about your ministry, how can you make sure you cover all the details? I fill out a contact sheet as we talk (see next page).

If the meeting planner schedules me immediately, I send along any requested information and then file this sheet in my folder labeled "Speaking Engagements" in order of the date of the event. When further correspondence comes in, I paper clip that information to the back of the contact sheet. Every time I talk to the meeting planner for that event, I pull out the contact sheet and make further notes.

If she does not schedule me immediately, I file this contact sheet in a folder labeled, "Potential Speaking Engagements." Then if she calls back, I can quickly pull out the sheet and remember the details. Later, if they do schedule me, it gets moved to the "Speaking Engagements" file.

Some speakers use a manila envelope to store these papers. Whatever method you use, use it consistently.

If I am not chosen for an event, I still have the meeting planner's name, address, and phone number so that I can send her an updated MIS in the future.

After an event, I log the meeting planner's name, organization, address, and phone number into a separate "mailing list" file for future use. Another possibility is to save the contact sheets. Recently, I went through my list of planners and sent them my updated Ministry Information Sheet. Some of those letters were returned because of invalid addresses, and I was able to update my file. On the positive side, I received several calls inviting me to speak again.

Contract

Once you've secured a speaking engagement, you may want to use a contract to solidify the details. I use the contract/agreement for most of my engagements, and request a deposit for most also. I've provided a sample contract on page 218.

Speaking Fees

This is a touchy part of speaking. Many people believe that speakers should not be paid at all, but Luke 10:7 says, "...for the worker

Speaking Engagements

Event Date_______________________ Initial Contact Date______________

Name of Church/Organization_____________________________________

Contact Person________________________ Heard from_______________

Address______________________________ Telephone_______________

Address of Place to Speak____

Telephone_____________

Time Begins & Ends__________________ Time I'll Be There______________

Type of Meeting__________________ Number of People Expected__________

Title of Speech___________________________ How Long to Speak________

Theme____

Meal(s) Included____

Needs: Book Table____

Someone to Attend Book Table______________________________________

Overhead Projector____

Accommodations ____

Handouts____

Transportation:____

Car____

Airport____

Airline Reservation____

Pick Up Person____

Fee Requested _______________________ Fee Promised________________

Sent: Date_________________

Ministry Information Sheet____

PR Tape____

Photo____

Agreement____

Speaker Appearance Agreement
For Kathy Collard Miller

This agreement confirms the speaking engagement of Kathy Collard Miller on (date) for (event type).

Financial Agreement:

Accommodations and Meals:

Travel:

Additional Requirements and/or Information:

[Example: Please provide a book table for the sale of Kathy's books and tapes. Kathy will supply change, books, and tapes. Kathy would appreciate an overhead projector and screen/wall being supplied for use during her presentations.]

Signature: Date:

Sponsor Signature: Date:

Sponsor:

Sponsoring Organization:

Address:

Business Phone:

Residence Phone:

Please sign both copies and return one copy to our office.
Thank you.

P.O. Box l058
Placentia CA 92871
7l4-993-2654; FAX: 714-993-1833
Kathy@larryandkathy.com
www.larryandkathy.com

deserves his wages." Being a speaker creates expenses like clothing, dry-cleaning, gas, car maintenance, postage, printing, telephone, as well as requiring time and energy. I don't think the Lord wants us to deduct those expenses from the welfare of our families. Few Christian speakers become rich. Yet, we do need to earn some money to cover our expenses and expand our materials.

In the beginning, a speaker's fees will be low. As a speaker learns her craft, it's appropriate for fees to increase. When a speaker's outreach is such that the demands on her time are beyond what she can handle, she can use higher fee requests as a way to speak to the largest possible group for the most efficient use of her time.

Marita Littauer, who advises and helps speakers develop their ministry through CLASS (Christian Leaders, Authors & Speakers Seminar), gives these guidelines for setting fees. "For the new, unknown speaker who hasn't published any books but has 'put in time,' I have found that a fee of between $100-250 for a single presentation, such as a luncheon or banquet, is normal and acceptable. For a multi-session engagement such as a one-day seminar or weekend retreat, $250-500 is appropriate. While it may not seem right to charge a group $250 for a single presentation and then do a four or five session retreat for $500, that is how it is done—somewhat like a package deal!"

She advises that the "mid-level" speaker who has several years of experience along with one or more books published, should command fees such as $300-500 for a single session and $500-1,000 for a weekend package.

For those on the "A" list who are nationally famous, fees starting at $1,000 are appropriate.

Quoted fees always mean "plus expenses," and it's wise to mention that when negotiating fees. An hour's driving time usually isn't reason to charge more, but beyond that, $.32 a mile can be charged. For events like retreats where the speaker must stay overnight, his or her meals and lodging should be provided.

When I'm contacted regarding a speaking engagement and the fee comes up, I handle it in this way. If the meeting planner asks, "What do you charge?" I ask, "What do you have available in your budget for your speaker?" If they quote more than I would have asked for, I thank them! If they quote less, then I say, "Well, I usually request $___ but I would be glad to receive that" (if I am). Sometimes, they may say, "We might be able to provide that amount."

If the suggestion is below what you'd request and the planner can't raise it, but you want to take the engagement, you could state, "I'm able to take a certain number of engagements free [or below my costs] as an offering [or tithe] to the Lord." If you do not want to take the engagement, you could say, "I'm able to take a certain number of engagements free [or below my costs] as an offering [or tithe] to the Lord, but I've already filled that quota for this year. Please feel free to try me again next year."

When I've taken the opportunities that didn't pay as well, I've seen the Lord's faithfulness in blessing me financially in other ways. Often my book sales will be particularly good, or I'll make a contact who asks me to speak at another function.

Quoting fees is never an easy aspect of our ministry, but you can determine what is appropriate for your level of experience and expertise. Then don't feel embarrassed to ask for it.

Clothing Choices

Knowing how to dress for different speaking engagements is an art. I don't consider myself an expert in fashion. In fact, I'm fashion-challenged. Yet, I still feel great when I go on my speaking engagements because I use the services of a friend who is a professional personal shopper.

Wise clothing choices must start with discovering your right color scheme. Since I did that many years ago, I've come a long way in being able to mix and match clothing. As a result, I don't have to buy as many outfits.

Generally, we should dress one notch above the dress standard of the group we're addressing. We want to stand out as the speaker and gain respect.

For instance, if I'm speaking at a weekend retreat in the mountains, even though everyone may wear jeans and slacks, I'll dress in a casual skirt and blouse or sweater. If it's a church women's group, I'll wear a suit. If it's a mothers' group in a home, I'll wear a dress with a linen jacket and flats. If it's a Friday night banquet, I'll put on a fancy dress.

By choosing our clothing carefully, we communicate the idea that our audience is important to us.

Visual Aids

I love using visual aids. The response I've received assures me they are valuable tools.

During my testimony talk, I tell about how I was so angry with my husband one day after he left our house through the laundry room door that I threw an apple at it (not him!). Shattered apple pieces flew all over the laundry room, adhering to the ceiling and the walls. That apple anecdote is a central theme of my talk: my life was shattered like that apple.

After sharing how God healed my life and my marriage, I hold up a half-eaten apple (don't worry, it's wooden), and ask the audience, "Do parts of your life seem like shattered pieces? Do you wonder whether God can put them back together again?" After a slight pause, I hold up a whole apple, and say, "This apple represents my life now. Although it's not perfect, God has done mighty things. I believe He wants to do the same for you: healing and restoring the shattered apple pieces of your life."

Sometimes when I arrive at a speaking engagement, someone will come up to me and say, "Oh, I've heard you before, you're the lady with the apples." I was thrilled to know that my apples had made an impact.

Other visual aids I use have been just as powerful. One is a cheesecloth that I use during my talk on problems. I wrap the cheesecloth around me saying that nothing can come into our lives—nothing can go through God's love filter—without His permission and plan for a good result.

Another tool is an index card that I pass out during my talk on worry. On one side, the audience writes in big letters, "STOP!" On the other side, they write out Proverbs 3:5-6, "Trust in the Lord with all your heart, And lean not on your own understanding; In all your ways acknowledge Him And He shall direct your paths" (NKJV). I instruct them to carry this card, and as soon as they recognize they are worrying, to say out loud "Stop!" and then repeat the verse. This can redirect their attention back to the Lord.

For my first talk at weekend retreats, I carry up to the podium a brightly decorated box containing my visual aids. I put it aside, hoping that I've captured the attention of my audience. At the end of that first presentation, which is usually my testimony, I'll rummage around in the box, pulling out whatever I'm going to use Saturday morning and say, "Oh, now why did I bring this? Oh, that's right, I'll talk about it tomorrow morning." Usually, the audience groans their disappointment. Then I tantalize them with something else. In my third try, I use the apples. Throughout the whole weekend, I tease them with something new each time I'm going to use a visual aid from the box. Believe me, whenever I reach for that box, I have their complete attention. I love it, and so do they!

I encourage you to develop your own line of visual aids. They are a significant way to help your audience remember the important things you have to say.

Handouts

Another way to augment the learning of your audience is to use handouts. Typically, these have an outline or a more detailed description so that your audience can take notes. Another plus in providing a handout puts your name, address, telephone number, and email address (printed on the bottom) accessible for future contact. Although I don't supply a handout at every presentation, 75 percent of the time I do.

Training Opportunities

None of us are perfect speakers; therefore, we must always be improving. Here are some organizations that offer training:

CLASS: Christian Leaders, Authors & Speakers Seminars

PO Box 66810, Albuquerque, NM 87193, Tel: 505-899-4283, www.classervices.com. CLASS provides a three-day seminar taught by author and speaker Florence Littauer and her daughter, Marita Littauer.

NSA: National Speakers Association

1500 South Priest Drive, Tempe, AZ 85281, Tel: 480-968-2552. This organization, although secular, has many Christians involved and provides seminars in different parts of the country to encourage speaker skills and networking.

Toastmasters International

P.O. Box 9052, Mission Viejo, CA 92688, Tel: 949-858-8255. Toastmasters has chapters throughout the United States and the world that meet for the specific purpose of offering instruction and opportunities to practice speeches.

Book Table

If you're a speaker and an author, then an added dimension to your speaking is selling your book(s). When my first book, *Help for Hurting Moms,* was published in 1984, I took a big box full to my next speaking engagement even though I knew there would only be twenty women there. My bubble burst when I only sold two books.

Now as I prepare for speaking engagements, I anticipate sales to be 10 percent of the audience, although I take extras. For retreats, sales increase because the audience has more opportunities to buy.

In the beginning, I hesitated mentioning the book table during my speeches. I feared appearing like a salesman. Then one Sunday evening, I heard a visiting speaker at our church mention a brief summary of one of his books. I thought, "That's what I've been looking for!" I bought his book, and it became a significant blessing in my life and inspired me to write my book, *Your View of God… God's View of You.*

I realized I needed to give the same courtesy to my audiences. How were they to know whether one of my books would be what they wanted unless I teased them with a short summary of ten seconds for each book? Since I have over forty books published, I usually just pick out three or four titles to mention quickly.

An idea that softens my "commercial" is an idea I learned from speaker and author Jeanne Zornes. After the short summary, I ask for the person whose birthday is closest to that day. Then I give her one of my books. Often the whole audience breaks into applause, and I lead them in singing "Happy Birthday."

You'll need to have change available. At first, I sold my books with the exact tax amount included. That meant the price was $7.37 or $9.49, and I had to bring a wide collection of coins. After carting around a heavy change box and noticing how long it took to make change, I rounded off my prices to the nearest quarter. That way I only have to carry quarters and bills (usually ones and fives). A basic rule of thumb is one dollar for every expected audience member.

I always ask my contact person for one or two people (or more for very large groups) to help me at the book table. That way I can concentrate on talking to people and giving my autograph while my helpers make change and stock inventory.

As far as indicating the price of books, I use a sign set up on the table. Other speakers and authors pencil in the price on the first page of each book.

Be sure to have copies of your MIS available on the book table. It's also a good idea to have ready (but not on the book table) an order form for your books and tapes. By passing it out only if asked, you won't encourage them to procrastinate in buying.

Even if you aren't a published author, you can still make a book table available with your MIS and books authored by others that pertain to your speaking topics. You could also write pamphlets and print out information sheets that share important details about the topics you cover.

I hope you'll enjoy interacting with the people at the book table as much as I do. Don't be timid about making your books available. That's why you've written them!

Record Keeping

Keeping records of your speaking ministry is a sometimes tedious chore but very important. I use a four-column business pad on which I list:

1. Speaking: How much I was paid.
2. Expenses: Any expenses that are deductible.
3. Sales: How much money I collected on book sales.
4. Royalties/Articles: Money received for royalties or article sales.

On each line I include the date of the transaction, where the money was spent, or how I received it. When I have book sales, on the next line under the name of the group I spoke to, I include: How many people were there, whether it was a retreat or more than one presentation, how many copies sold of each book, and the number of tapes that sold. This accounting comes in handy as a reference for how much might sell when I'm speaking before a similar-sized group.

Before taking any checks to the bank, I write down the name and address, which can be used for future mailings. In the past, one of my publishers printed postcards about my new book, and I mailed out announcements to those on my mailing list.

As a business person, you'll need to pay the taxes you collected on your books to your state Board of Equalization. Getting a license with them will also entitle you to buy your books, tapes, and tape covers without paying tax. Check in your telephone book for the local Board of Equalization office.

Of course, we can't forget our obligation to the government. Keep accurate records for them including the mileage you drove. Since we don't have federal or state taxes taken out of our earnings, we have to pay taxes usually in quarterly filings. It's wise to lay some aside for that. Also, check into whether you need to pay toward the Social Security tax. If you don't have someone knowledgeable to advise you of these details, consult an accountant.

The important and powerful speaking ministry God has given us is a privilege and delight. Although there are some aspects of it that seem unrelated (like bookkeeping), it's all a part of the package of sharing the message that God has given us. So take it in stride and don't let any of these "business side of speaking" aspects sidetrack you from proclaiming God's truth.

21 Puting Power in Your Presentation

by Marita Littauer

As speakers we are always on stage, just as Christians we are always sharing Christ.

—Florence Littauer

I have been teaching people how to speak though the CLASSeminars since 1981. As those in the audience watch me and the other staff members interact with each other on the platform, they can see we are having fun. They watch us flex with the schedule and add in stories of events that just took place during the previous break. They see that we have few or no notes.

As the afternoon winds down, and we are nearing the part of the schedule where each participant goes to his small group to prepare and deliver a presentation, the anxiety level rises. After comparing those who are up front with the attendees in the small groups, I am often asked, "Will it ever become fun for me?"

Admittedly, there are those of us who are more naturally hams, those whose personalities gravitate toward the stage. Yet, everyone, regardless of personality, can become an effective speaker, can enjoy being up front, and can put power in a presentation. After a while, it does become fun!

The concepts presented in this chapter are repeatedly those voted the most helpful at the CLASSeminars. Here you will learn how to take a diverse selection of thoughts and ideas and bring them together to create a powerful presentation—either spoken or written—that will be easy for you to prepare and effectively communicate to the listener or reader. Actually sitting down and putting everything together is where many people get stuck. They have a few ideas they wish to communicate, but they do not know how to pull it all together.

Having these skills will be an asset to you no matter what you do in life, even if you never plan to give a speech. The book, *Business Protocol: How to Survive and Succeed in Business* quotes a manager as saying, "People who can express themselves clearly are at an advantage. This goes beyond using good grammar, proper spelling, and appropriate diction in all your communications; you must also speak and write to the point."

There are five parts to putting power in your presentation. These steps will make it easy for you to put it all together—and make it easier for your audience to understand and remember the key ideas you wish to communicate.

Passion

Many people think being a speaker looks like a glamorous lifestyle. They ask, "How can I become a speaker?" I believe you don't really become a speaker, rather it is an evolution. You don't one day decide, "I'd like to be a speaker," then check out books, learn jokes, use other people's material, and reprocess it all into a speech you call your own.

Some may have excellent acting skills and be able to pull this off. But, for most their message is empty. You can tell when you listen to these people that something doesn't ring true. You can probably think of people you have heard who have done this. You can learn everything else, but you cannot learn the passion.

Start by examining your own life. What are you so excited about that you can't keep quiet? For those who desire to be Christian speakers, what has God done in your life lately that you want to share? These are your passions. They are things that are a natural outpouring of who you are and what you believe. When you start with a passion, the other important pieces fall into place much more easily. Glenna Salsbury, former President of the National Speakers Association, advises, "Your purpose should be larger than your speaking career. Speaking should be a vehicle to fulfill your purpose. Every time you give a presentation, is it springing from your purpose? If so, you are unforgettable on the platform."

Personal Examples

I have been involved in teaching others to be more effective speakers for many years. As a result, I listen to other speakers differently from the average audience member. When I see speakers who are nervous or struggling, I want to help them. I have seen countless speakers who start out nervously fidgeting with their pens or the change in their pockets, and peppering their words with an abundance of "ah" and "and ah."

As I watch, hurting for the presenter, I have discovered an almost universal cure for the pain—both the speaker's and mine. As soon as the speaker begins to share a personal story, something he or she knows backwards and forwards, something he doesn't need notes to tell, he warms up. He becomes more natural and animated as he tells stories from his own life.

Personal examples add energy to your message. They let the audience know you have been there and that you know what you are talking about. Be sure to use them liberally throughout your presentation.

Preparation

This next point is the most important, and therefore we will spend the most time here. Passion and personal examples are valuable tools, but if you don't prepare, you may gush on enthusiastically with no real point or purpose.

The key to preparation is to know your subject well, know what ideas you wish to communicate. Yet be flexible enough to adjust some of your material to fit the specific needs of each group and the required time frame.

When I was first beginning to speak, my mother told me I should have ten hours of information in my head for every one hour I was going to speak. While that may seem a bit extreme, it does ensure that you *do* know your subject well!

Many novice speakers are afraid that when they stand up in front of all those people, their minds will go blank. As a result, they write out their speeches word for word. When they stand up front they actually read the entire message. Most likely you have heard some of these types of speakers.

It is obvious when someone is reading a speech. I always feel offended that I took my time to attend a program where the speaker is reading a speech. I feel like that person could have just mailed out the script, and I could have done something else with my time.

In Toastmasters International, the group that meets weekly to help people improve their speaking skills, the last assignment in the first level program is to write out your speech word for word and deliver it following those notes exactly. This assignment is last because it is the most difficult, yet this is where many people start.

Instead, preparing your speech in the method I suggest will allow you to have everything you need in front of you, in case your mind goes blank, yet offers flexibility. Notice the term "preparing a presentation" rather than "writing."

A good speech should not be written out word for word. It should be "prepared" with all of the key ideas, teaching, stories, and Scripture in the notes—all of which you follow for continuity. But, by not writing it out word for word, you allow for flexibility in timing, group make-up, and the leading of the Holy Spirit as to the needs for this particular group.

The PIER System

The PIER system allows for all of these factors. PIER is an acronym for Point, Instruction, Example, and Reference. To help remember the concepts, think of yourself standing in front of an audience. You look out at them, and they look back at you like a sea of faces. The desire is to make your presentation stick out in their minds like a PIER sticks out into the ocean. By remembering "Point, Instruction, Example, and Reference," the speaker can be assured that all the ingredients needed for an effective presentation are available, but they are arranged to allow for flexibility.

Point

As you begin your speech preparation, start with the main ideas you wish to convey to your audience. These ideas, when collected together, become the *points* of your outline—the "P" of your PIER. As you sit down to prepare your presentation, say to yourself, "What are the key things I want the audience to remember?"

Let's say you get three ideas. On three separate pieces of paper write one idea across the top of each one. At this place in your preparation, your ideas may come to you in the form of a question, a single word, a thought, or a complete sentence. Don't worry about that yet. Simply write down the ideas as they come into your head.

Since you are writing each point on a separate piece of paper, it doesn't matter if they are in the order in which you will ultimately use them. Often, once you get into your preparation, you may decide that the point you had as the first one should be somewhere else. Since they are on separate pieces of paper, you can just rearrange them as you see fit.

About two inches down from your point, write an "I" in the margin on each piece of paper. Another two inches down write an "E" and another two inches an "R." This creates a simple fill-in-the-blanks form for your speech preparation.

Instruction

Think about your point. How are the listeners going to make that concept a part of their lives? These ideas become your instruction. For example, in your point you may tell your audience that having a good prayer life is important. In the *instruction* you will offer them several ways to improve their prayer life. Next to the "I" on your paper, write down the main techniques you want the audience to learn.

Since these ideas are from your head and should be something you have studied or experienced, they will be concepts you know well. Therefore, you don't have to write out long cumbersome instructions. By listing just the key steps, you can glance at your notes and be reminded of the things you intend to communicate. This way you can be sure to include all the concepts while you are standing in front of the audience.

Depending on the time allowed for the presentation, you may give detailed instruction and even have the audience try your suggestions right there, or you may simply give them the techniques to implement your ideas. Offering the listeners an idea without equipping them to accomplish it, will be frustrating to the audience and futile for you.

Example

If you give the listeners a point and then tell them how to do it but quit there, you may come across as preachy and unrelatable. To show the audience that you know what you're talking about, that you've been there, include a personal story that exemplifies the principle. You may share your own struggle with the situation and show how you overcame it, or the example given may be that of a friend or family member. People remember stories better than just points.

Again, these stories are usually things you have experienced so you won't need to write them out word for word. Next to the "E" on your notes, jot down a few key words to remind you which stories you intended to tell with that point. If you have a lot of time, you may want to include several stories to make your point. Or, if your time is cut at the last minute, which often happens, you can pare your stories down and just tell one or even use an abbreviated version if necessary.

You can also adjust your stories so they are appropriate for the particular audience you are addressing at the time. If the group is made up of men and women, be sure to use stories that will relate to both. If it is all women, you may use slightly different examples. They will feel as though you customized the presentation just for them. The stories will give your points life!

Reference

So far all we have discussed are your own ideas. The *reference* allows you to back up what you are saying and give it more authority. If your presentation is being given to a Christian audience, it should include various Scriptures. These would be your references.

This is where Bible software is useful. Personally, I recommend Bible Explorer (available from Epiphany Software). For a minimal investment, you can type in the word or topic you are looking for and tell it to search in the King James Version, Living or New Living, or Thompson's Chain Reference. With one click, you will find all the verses in the Bible that include your word or all the verses on the topic. With another click, you are at the verse. You can simply cut and paste the selection into your text.

You may have one verse you will want to quote or even several which will validate your point. Next to the "R" on your notes, list the Scripture reference of the verse or verses you wish to use.

If you are only using a couple of verses you may want to write them out completely in your notes or copy them from the software if your worksheet is in the computer. Then you can quote them without having to fumble through your Bible while you are up front.

If your time is cut, you can simply offer the audience the Scripture reference you are using and paraphrase it to save time. If you have been asked to stretch your message, which does rarely happen, you could give the reference and ask someone from the audience to find the verse and read to the group.

In addition to the Bible there are many other references you can use to reinforce what you are saying. They may include newspaper or magazine articles and books. Beyond your own reading and research, another excellent resource is *Current Thoughts and Trends*, a publication produced monthly by the Navigators. This beneficial periodical summarizes the important articles, statistics, and news from more than seventy-five Christian and key secular magazines. Originally designed for pastors, *Current Thoughts and Trends* will help you stay up to date and well informed on issues and topics of interest.

When you quote from a magazine article, have the actual article in your hand and read from it. Having the visual stimulation adds variety for the audience and affirms your source. If you have collected the articles with the cover, as suggested in the previous chapter, show the cover briefly as you read the article. If your eyesight is such that reading the fine print while you are standing in front of a group is difficult, write the quotation on a large Post-it® note and place it inside the magazine cover so you still have the appearance of reading the actual article.

Additionally, I recommend that all speakers have a good quotation book such as *Bartlett's Familiar Quotations* in their resource libraries. The Internet also offers many sites with searchable databases of quotations. When you do use these additional references, be sure to have their source in your notes. You don't have to include the source in the verbal presentation, but you should have it in case anyone questions its validity.

After you have filled in all your blanks, the next step is to make your points easier to remember. You, as the speaker, will have notes from which to work. Therefore you could give your presentation with one point being a question, another being a single word, and another being a thought. However, when there is no continuity to your points, they are not as clear for your audience to catch or as easy for them to remember. Once the hard part is done, you are ready to polish your presentation.

Go back over your points. If, for example, three are questions and one is a single word, can you rework the idea the single word represents into a question so the points are uniform? Or, if there is no obvious pattern to your points, try to boil the points down to one or two words that represent the main thought.

Review your points again. Do several of them start with the same letter? Do a couple of them rhyme? Or, can you use the first letters to spell a word that summarizes the focus of your overall message? If you see an emerging pattern, try to make the other points fit that pattern. This is where a thesaurus or synonym finder is helpful. Personally, I would be lost without J.I. Rodale's *The Synonym Finder*. If you have one or two words that don't fit the pattern, look them up and see if you can find a synonym, which will communicate the same point but fit within your pattern.

For example, here are three real points I often use to teach this concept. These points originally came from an article on father/daughter relationships by Gary Smalley. His points are: 1) A father should include meaningful touching as his daughter grows up. 2) A father who wants to develop a close relationship with his daughter should invest himself in her best interest. 3) A father should keep his anger under control.

Now quickly cover up that paragraph and try to repeat those points without looking. You can't, can you? While those are three excellent points, they are too long and cumbersome to be easily remembered. Let's look at the first point. 1) A father should include meaningful touching as his daughter grows up. Can you condense it down to one key word? How about "Touch"?

Now let's look at the second point. 2) A father who wants to develop a close relationship with his daughter should invest himself in her best interest. Now there are several key words you could pick out, but since the word we have chosen for the first point begins with a "T," can you think of a "T" word that captures the heart of that point? How about "Time?"

Okay, the last point. 3) A father should keep his anger under control. What "T" word comes to mind for this one? Most people come up with Temper. Yes, that is a "T" word and it does capture the essence of the point, but does it work? Check your points once you have simplified them. They should all be the same parts of speech: all nouns, all verbs, all thoughts, all sentences, or all questions.

To check this you can simply put a prefix before the point. You might say, "A daughter needs Touch." "A daughter needs Time." Those both work. Point number three, "A daughter needs Temper." How can you rework that so that it fits the context, is a "T" word, and is the correct part of speech? Tenderness: "A daughter needs Tenderness." Now you have three easy to remember points—Touch, Time, and Tenderness. The message is the same, but now it is also easy to remember.

Presentation

PIER works for any type of teaching presentation. Once you have filled out your "form" using the PIER formula, you have your speech basically prepared. When you are ready to actually present your message, you will need an opening, perhaps a story—the "E" in PIER—which will put you at ease.

Or, it may be a question that helps to create a need in the audience for your subject. If you do begin with a question, be sure that it is a question with an obvious answer and one that everyone present can answer affirmatively, without embarrassment. This same principle is true for any questions you might ask throughout the presentation. Additionally, questions where you want the audience members to stand up and share a lengthy answer are best used in a workshop setting, not a keynote presentation.

When I begin my presentation on "Personality Puzzle," I always ask the audience, "How many of you have noticed there are people out there who are different from you?" Of course everyone has noticed that. So they can all answer by raising their hands in agreement. To indicate that I am expecting a response to the question, and particularly a raised hand, I raise my hand as I lean into the audience and ask the question.

By asking a question to which they can all respond, I have already done several things. First, I have created an atmosphere of interaction. Rather than having a sense of being preached at, the audience is already involved. Also, since the question is something that applies to everyone, the communal response draws the audience together.

After your opening story, question, or questions, move right into your points. Remember, PIER is a formula, not usually an outline in itself. However, if the speech only has one point, PIER could become your outline. By preparing your presentation using PIER, you have all the information you need. But, when you actually present it, you can start with the story (the example), and then move into the point you learned from the story, then teach the audience how to apply that in their own lives (the instruction), and then wrap that point up with a quotation or Scripture. You can arrange the point, instruction, example, and reference any way you want, and you can present it differently each time.

If you choose to use a handout for your presentation—which I suggest, as it allows your audience to follow along and provides them with a place to take notes—use the points of this outline to make up your handout. If you are using Scriptures or quotations, you may also want to include them in a smaller font. This prevents losing people as they lean over to the person next to them and ask, "What verse was that?"

By including the chapter and verses on the handout, you can skip them in a really tight time situation, but still allow the people to have that valuable part of your presentation. However, do not tell the audience your time has been cut, or that you are out of time, simply say, "I have included some special Bible verses on your handout for you to use as a study guide when you get home." That way it looks like you had planned it that way along!

If you do choose to use a handout, be sure to include your name, address, phone number, and email address to identify whose material the audience is taking home. This way if they want to quote you at a later date or use your ideas in some research of their own, they know how to find you to get permission. Plus, if they love what you said and want to recommend you to another group, they will know how to contact you.

Finally, you will need a closing, which may include a recapping or a summary of your points and then end with a challenge or call to commitment. Often a poem or other inspirational piece that exemplifies your message is an effective closing. The closing poem doesn't have to be an original composition. However, if you are gifted in poetry, this is an excellent place to incorporate it. If the closing quotation or poem is not original, be sure to cite the source.

Many people who are giving a Christian message in a church type setting feel as though they should close with prayer. Unless the presentation is an actual sermon, I suggest that you not use a prayer as your final words. Closing with a prayer in a non-church service setting confuses the audience.

In our society, the way we show appreciation to a person who is on the "stage"—a performer, singer, or speaker—is by applause. This lets you know you did a good job and is the audience's way of thanking you. However, closing in prayer creates a somber and quiet mood. We are not accustomed to breaking into applause at the sound of "Amen." So when you close with prayer, the audience doesn't know whether they should thank you with applause or keep quiet. It creates an awkward and uncomfortable moment for everyone.

If a prayer of confession or commitment is appropriate after your presentation, there are two effective ways to handle it. One is that you can have the emcee or program chairman do it after you have finished. Or, you can offer the prayer that is on your heart. But then come back with your summary of points, closing poem, or concluding challenge. This provides an effective transition from the prayer mood to a powerful closing and will leave your audience on an up note.

Occasionally, the desired mood may be a quiet somber exit into a time of reflection or stillness. In such circumstances, the prayer may be the most effective way to close.

One of the other benefits of using PIER to prepare your speech—rather than writing it out word for word—is that you allow for other changes as well. Sometimes the group is not who you expected it to be. With PIER you have the ability to make quick changes without panicking!

Additionally, PIER more easily allows for the Holy Spirit's direction based on the needs of the group. When you have prepared your speech rather than writing it out, you can have variations without feeling stress. Sometimes I find myself saying words that I had not intended to say or sharing a story that was not in my notes. As I say the words, part of my brain is asking, "Where did that come from? That is not what I usually say here."

Almost always, someone comes up to me afterwards and says, "You know what you said about…? You said that for me. It was just what I needed to hear today." Thank you Holy Spirit!

Practice

The final thing you need to do is practice. Once you have found the subject area of your passion, peppered it with the vitality of personal examples, prepared your message, and put the presentation together, you are ready to practice. Start alone in your bedroom or office, preferably in front of a full-length mirror. Allow that passion to show and use hand gestures to clarify your points.

Work on your message until you are comfortable with all the parts, then tape-record it. Listen to how you sound. You are apt to find places where you have lots of gap fillers such as "ah" and "you know." These usually indicate an area where you are not as familiar with your material or are not comfortable with it. Study those areas and make changes.

While it is unlikely you will ever be completely happy with your finished product, the next thing is to give your speech in front of supportive, but honest friends and/or family. This may be three people in your living room, or it may be your Bible study group at your church. Ask for their encouragement and insight. Notice I didn't say criticism. Accept their praise and listen to their suggestions.

If they suggest many changes, you may want to give your speech once more in a controlled environment before you venture beyond the safety of your support network. If they give you a thumbs up, go on. Share what God has put on your heart with others—and expect results!

When you prepare your speech using the PIER system you can be confident that you have included everything you need for a strong presentation and still have the freedom and flexibility that is the sign of a pro.

Appendix

The Christian Communicator Manuscript Critique Service

Once you have finished your book proposal, if you would like to have your manuscript critiqued to make it more professional before sending it to a publisher, send it to the Christian Communicator Manuscript Critique Service.

One of our fourteen editors will critique your manuscript, offer ideas for improvement, and suggest markets when possible.

Fees Are:

Articles and Stories	**$70**
Three-chapter Book Proposals	**$100**
Children's Picture Books	**$70**
Additional Editing (per hour)	**$25**

The average book proposal includes a query letter, a brief chapter synopsis for nonfiction or a running synopsis for a novel, and three sample chapters (usually the first three). If you would like your entire book critiqued, send your manuscript with a check payable to Susan Titus Osborn for $105, and we will give you an estimate on the balance before finishing the critique. Don't forget to include an SASE, if you don't include the $5. We will give you a line-by-line critique as well as an overall evaluation.

Mail manuscript, check, and SASE to:

Susan Titus Osborn
3133 Puente Street
Fullerton CA 92835
714-990-1532
Susanosb@aol.com
www.christiancommunicator.com

Six-Session Hands-On Class

Available by Email

If you are just beginning, I'd recommend that you start by writing articles and stories. If you join the hands-on class, you will receive personal direction from Susan Titus Osborn. You can learn to write for publication while sitting in your home or office, using your own timetable.

Course includes the following lessons:

1. **Basics of Writing for Publication**
2. **Research, Structure, and Organization**
3. **Leads, Titles, Grammar, and Word Usage**
4. **Fiction Tips, Dialogue, and Characters**
5. **Query Letters, Manuscript Submission**
6. **Markets, Rights, Copyright Law**

Cost: $120

Six session email course:
Includes six lessons online, handouts, and critiqued assignments.
By the lesson: $25 per lesson

Completion of entire writing course entitles you to one unit of Continuing Education Credit (CEU) from Hope International University for an additional $30.

Mail check to:

Susan Titus Osborn
3133 Puente Street
Fullerton CA 92835
714-990-1532
Susanosb@aol.com
www.christiancommunicator.com

About the Authors

Marlene Bagnull has made more than one thousand sales to Christian periodicals and is the author of seven books, including the new, expanded version of *Write His Answer: A Bible Study for Christian Writers* (ACW Press). Marlene is the founder and director of the Greater Philadelphia Christian Writers' Conference. She also directs the Colorado Christian Writers' Conference, speaks at Christian writers' conferences around the nation, gives Write His Answer seminars, and teaches a correspondence study program for Christian writers called the At-Home Writing Workshops. You may reach her at 316 Blanchard Road, Drexel Hill, PA 19026, or via email at mbagnull@aol.com or visit her Web site at www.writehisanswer.com.

Donna Clark Goodrich is a freelance writer, editor, and proofreader who lives in Mesa, Arizona with her husband Gary. The author of twenty books and more than seven hundred short stories and articles, she began the annual Arizona Christian Writers Seminar in 1981 and has since taught at conferences across the United States. To contact Donna, email dgood648@aol.com.

Dr. Dennis E. Hensley is director of the professional writing major at Taylor University Fort Wayne, where he is an associate professor of English. For the 2001-2002 academic year, he was named "Distinguished Visiting Professor of Journalism and English" in the graduate school of Regent University. His thirty-one books include *Teach Yourself Grammar and Style in 24 Hours* (Macmillan) and *How to Write What You Love and Make a Living at It* (Harold Shaw/Random House), both released in 2000. He is a contributing editor with six national magazines. He holds four degrees in communications, including a Ph.D. in English from Ball State University, where he was named "Distinguished Doctoral Graduate in English."

Mona Gansberg Hodgson has nineteen children's books published, including the "Desert Critter Series," the "I Wonder Series", and *Hide and Seek*, a devotional book. She's had several hundred fillers, poems, articles, and short stories for adults and children printed in more than fifty periodicals. In addition to writing, teaching at writers' conferences, and speaking to school groups and at women's retreats, Mona serves as director of the Glorieta Christian Writers' Conference in Glorieta, New Mexico. She is a member of Christian Writers' Fellowship International; The Society of Southwestern Authors; and the Faith, Hope, & Love Chapter of Romance Writers of America. She is also a graduate of the CLASSeminar. Contact Mona by email at mona@sedona.net or visit her Web site at www.desertcritters.com.

Marita Littauer is the President of CLASServices Inc. She has helped thousands of men and women enhance their personal and professional communication skills for both the spoken and written word. Marita is a professional speaker with more than twenty years of experience speaking to women's groups, church conferences, conventions, and businesses. She has authored ten books. *Personality Puzzle, Getting Along with Almost Anybody,* and *Talking So People Will Listen* were written with her mother, Florence Littauer. *Love Extravagantly,* her newest book, is written with her husband, Chuck Noon. They live in Albuquerque, New Mexico. For more information on Marita, CLASS, or the resources mentioned in "Putting Power in Your Presentation" please call 800-433-6633, email: info@classervices.com, or visit her Web site at www.classervices.com.

Kathy Collard Miller is the author of more than forty books including the best-selling *God's Vitamin "C" for the Spirit, Why Do I Put So Much Pressure on Myself?,* and *Through His Eyes.* She speaks thirty to fifty times a year and has spoken in twenty-four states and four foreign countries. She can be reached at kathy@larryandkathy.com or see her Web site at www.larryandkathy.com.

Cecil ("Cec") Murphey has published more than eighty books and just signed his eighty-fifth book contract. A full-time writer, he has published fiction and nonfiction books and has been a ghostwriter for celebrities such as Dr. Ben Carson, Franklin Graham, and pianist Dino Karsanakas. His book, *Gifted Hands* (Zondervan), has been in print since 1990, and sales have exceeded a million copies. He also writes books under his own name, such as *Seeking God's Hidden Face* (InterVarsity Press, 2000) and *Encountering the Holy* (Bethany, 2001). Contact Cec at Cec_Haraka@email.msn.com.

Susan Titus Osborn is director of the Christian Communicator Manuscript Critique Service. She is a contributing editor of *The Christian Communicator* and *The Galilean.* Susan is also an adjunct professor at Hope International University in Fullerton, California. She has authored twenty-seven books and hundreds of articles. Susan is a publisher's representative for Broadman & Holman

Publishers and Concordia Publishing House, and she is a CLASS Speaker. She has taught at over 125 writers' conferences across the US and in five foreign countries. She is listed in Marquis *Who's Who in America, Who's Who of American Women, Who's Who in the World, Who's Who in the West,* and *Who's Who in the Media and Communications.* Contact her at 3133 Puente Street, Fullerton CA 92835 or email Susanosb@aol.com. See her Web site at www.christiancommunicator.com.

Carole Gift Page, a prolific author of forty-three books and eight hundred stories and articles, has published both fiction and nonfiction with a dozen major Christian publishers, including Thomas Nelson, Moody Press, Crossway Books, Bethany House, Tyndale House, and Harvest House. An award-winning novelist, Carole has received the C.S. Lewis Honor Book Award and been a finalist several times for the prestigious Gold Medallion Award and the Campus Life Book of the Year Award. Her most recent releases are *Becoming a Woman of Passion* (Fleming Revell), *Misty* (Spire Books), and the "Minister's Daughters" series (three romance novels, by Steeple Hill). You may contact Carole at cgiftpag@jps.net.

Mary Carpenter Reid is the author of seventeen books, including the "Backpack Mystery" series of early readers for Bethany House Publishers. Her work has appeared in secular and Christian adult and juvenile publications. Mary has critiqued hundreds of manuscripts and operates her own editorial service. She can be reached at marycreid@aol.com.

Lee Roddy was a staff writer for a motion picture and television production company and a newspaper editor and publisher before becoming a best-selling author. He has written fifty-one juvenile and adult novels and fifteen nonfiction books. Millions of his books have been sold in the U.S. and in eighteen foreign countries. *Grizzly Adams* became a prime-time TV series, *The Lincoln Conspiracy* made the New York Times best-seller list, and *Jesus* is now a film in more than five hundred languages through Campus Crusade. His main readers are boys, ages eight to twelve. For more information, log onto www.leeroddybooks.com.

Gayle G. Roper loves stories and has authored more than thirty books, her latest being *Spring Rain* (Multnomah) and *Riding the Waves* (Broadman & Holman). *Caught in a Bind* (Zondervan) won the Holt Medallion award for best long inspirational romance of 2000, and *The Decision* (Multnomah) won the Holt Medallion for the best short inspirational romance of 1999. Her articles have appeared in numerous periodicals, including *Discipleship Journal, Moody Magazine,* and *The Christian Communicator.* She also loves speaking at writers' conferences and women's events. She adores her kids and grandkids and loves her own personal patron of the arts, her husband Chuck. She may be reached at Ggroper@aol.com.

Nancy I. Sanders is the author of fifty books. She has written for such publishers as Concordia Publishing House, Tyndale House Publishers, Scholastic Professional Books, and Reader's Digest Books for Young Readers. She lives in Chino Hills, California with her husband, Jeff, and two teenage sons, Dan and Ben. She welcomes email at JNDBSand@peoplepc.com.

Dr. Lowell S. Saunders taught college courses for thirty years. He has authored twenty-two books and more than 450 articles. He is known as "Doc" to his friends by virtue of his Ph.D. in Communication from the University of Illinois. Now in official retirement, he remains active as a visiting minister for the Reformed Episcopal Church. He makes his home in Frazier Park, California with his wife, Carole.

Jessica Shaver has had poetry published in *Moody Magazine, Purpose, Inklings, Time of Singing, Living Streams, Japan Times, The Christian Communicator, People Plus* and the *South Coast Poetry Journal.* Her book *Gianna: Aborted and Lived to Tell About It* (Focus on the Family, 1995), was a Gold Medallion finalist. Jessica's email is Litlshaver@aol.com.

Sally E. Stuart has published more than nine hundred articles and twenty-eight books, including *Sally Stuart's Guide to Getting Published* and *The Christian Writers' Market Guide.* A leading authority on Christian publishing, she currently writes for *The Christian Communicator* and *The Advanced Christian Writer.* Sally is also a popular speaker at writers' conferences nationwide. Contact Sally at 1647 SW Pheasant Dr., Aloha OR 97006, or email stuartcwmg@aol.com.

Christine Harder Tangvald has authored eighty picture books for children. She currently has over 2.5 million books in print in eight languages. She has taught at seventy-five secular and Christian writers' conferences throughout the U.S. She has also written greeting cards, curriculum, devotions, stories, and articles for many publications. Her book *Easter Is For Me* (Bethany House Publishers) was number one on the CBA best-selling list in May 2001. She and her husband live in Spokane, Washington.

W. Terry Whalin is a Feature Writer for Christianity.com. He has written for more than fifty publications and published more than fifty books including *Prayers for My Son, Prayers for My Daughter,* and *Lessons from the Pit.* His Web site with a series of automatic helps for writers is located at www.terrywhalin.com.

Order Form

TITLE	PRICE	QTY
The Complete Guide to Christian Writing and Speaking —Susan Osborn	**$15.00**	____
A Complete Guide to Writing for Publication —Susan Osborn	**$15.00**	____
How to Write and Sell a Christian Novel —Gilbert Morris	**$12.00**	____
Introduction to Christian Writing —Ethel Herr	**$17.00**	____
Just Write —Susan Osborn	**$12.00**	____
Write His Answer —Marlene Bagnull	**$12.00**	____
	Subtotal $	__________
	Plus Shipping* $	__________
	TOTAL $	__________

Postal orders: 5501 N. 7th, #502, Phoenix, AZ 85013

Telephone orders: 800-931-BOOK

Name: ____

Address: ____

City: ______________________ State: ________

Zip: __________ Telephone: (_____) ________________

Order from:
Write Now Publications

or contact your local bookstore

***Shipping:** $3.00 for the first book and $1.00 for each additional book to cover shipping and handling within US, Canada, and Mexico. International orders add $6.00 for the first book and $2.00 for each additional book.